THE *THINKING CLEARLY* SERIES

Series editor: Clive Calver

The *Thinking Clearly* series sets out the main issues in a variety of important subjects. Written from a mainstream Christian standpoint, the series combines clear biblical teaching with up-to-date scholarship. Each of the contributors is an authority in his or her field. The series is written in straightforward everyday language, and each volume includes a range of practical applications and guidance for further reading.

The series has two main aims:
1. To help Christians understand their faith better
2. To show how Christian truths can illuminate matters of crucial importance in our society.

THE *THINKING CLEARLY* SERIES

Series Editor: Clive Calver

Thinking Clearly About
Truth

CLIVE CALVER

MONARCH
EVANGELICAL ALLIANCE

British Library Cataloguing Data
A catalogue record for this book is available
from the British Library.

ISBN 1 85424 289 X

Co-published with the Evangelical Alliance,
Whitefield House, 186 Kennington Park Road,
London SE11 4BT.

Produced by Bookprint Creative Services
P.O. Box 827, BN21 3YJ, England for
MONARCH PUBLICATIONS
Broadway House, The Broadway,
Crowborough, East Sussex, TN6 1HQ.
Printed in Great Britain.

To Alex Buchanan and Lyndon Bowring – trusted friends
who have told me the truth about myself;
even when it hurt!

Contents

Foreword

People frequently ask me about my political and Christian views; usually in the context of how the two relate. In particular they want to know what I think about Christianity – what it means and what it means to me. Some seem to be motivated by the thought that being a Christian and a politician is an impossible combination! If so, they are wrong; as the many fine Christians of all political persuasions prove.

As part of these discussions, two questions constantly recur. Sometimes they stem from a genuine sense of enquiry. On other occasions they sound defensive, occasionally defiant, as if the questioner is preparing to defend his or her comfortable adaption of fundamental Christian truth against what they suspect will be my differing view.

When asked how I define a Christian, my answer is always the same. A Christian is not defined in the Bible as someone who is better than others in a moral sense, more loving than others in an ethical sense or more churchgoing than others in a religious sense – though in descriptive terms they should be all of these. A Christian is defined as someone who is forgiven – whose sins God has forgiven through the sacrifice of Jesus Christ – as Paul told the early Church in his letters.

It is that truth which makes the Christian faith unique. Forgiveness in the context of a relationship with the living Christ, son of the living God, is an awesome yet simple truth, which can change individuals, communities, the world.

The second question is similar to the first. It comes in a form something like, 'How can you tell if a person is a Christian?' My response is always to refer to John's Gospel. He describes Jesus –

the incarnate Word – as being full of grace and truth. It is the combination which is defining.

Too often in today's Christian world this pairing becomes split. Some focus on truth with a vehemence which drives people away from the good news of the Christian faith. Others proclaim a religion which is so gracious, so easy, as to be woolly and without sound foundation. As such it deprives the seeker of the certainty of faith.

Perhaps, because of my job, I have sensitivity about truth. Politics is about truth. It is also, powerfully, about people's perception of the truth. Elections can be won or lost, careers made or broken on the basis of an effective, simple idea or on the biased portrayal of a position.

Overwhelmingly our politicians are honourable men and women. They do wish to serve their constituents by framing laws that will be to their benefit. They try to persuade, frequently with passion, that what they propose is more likely to promote the common good than are the ideas of others. Of such is the essence of our democracy – a market place of good ideas, good works and good intentions based on what we believe and seek to portray as true.

The reason we disagree is because we start with different presuppositions. Our truth is not absolute. Because of this we all – practitioners, supporters, opponents and citizens alike – need to remember the words of St Thomas Aquinas: 'Political life neither provides our final end nor contains the happiness we seek for ourselves or others… The purpose of temporal tranquillity, which well-ordered policies establish and maintain, is to give opportunities for contemplating truth'.

Or to paraphrase St John: only Jesus Christ can change fundamentally a person's life.

Exploring that truth is what this book is all about.

My friendship with Clive Calver spans many years and has many roots. His commitment to the Christian good news is widely appreciated, as is his ability to explain it in a helpful, careful and winsome way. If you think I exaggerate because he is my friend, read this book. It makes the case. Grace and truth come together in a compelling and challenging way.

And remember, it was St Paul who wrote 'Whatsoever things are true … think on those things'.

Rt Hon Dr Brian Mawhinney, MP

Preface

Rarely is a book ever the total work of any one individual person – and this volume is no exception to the rule. Writing this Preface gives me the opportunity to express my sincere gratitude to all those who have worked to greatly enhance my own slim efforts. Thanks are due to many people:

* To Mark Birchall, Paul Hansford and Martyn Eden for their hours of work in refining both the argument and the text.
* To the staff at Monarch for editing and publishing the book.
* To friends like Lyndon Bowring, Nigel Cameron, Elaine Storkey, Steve Chalke, R.T. Kendall and Pete Broadbent for their advice, corrections and endorsement.
* To Tony Collins for initiating and encouraging, it has been a joy and privilege to work with him.
* To Janie Ewing for the patient hours of typing and correcting the manuscript.
* To John Hunt for his painstaking proof reading.
* To Steve and Ruth Chilcraft for extending their customary Spring Harvest research and hospitality to cover the production of this work as well.
* To the family – Ruth, Vicky, Kris, Gavin and Suzy for releasing me to write, and coping with the frustrations of a beleaguered author!

The influences on my thinking have been innumerable. Twelve years at the Evangelical Alliance has exposed me to so many different perspectives. I am grateful to all those who have helped me to understand that people have become intolerant with intolerance, and that this has put Christians at odds with much of contemporary society.

David Hilborn, Michael Schluter, George Russell, and Peter Meadows have all helped me with material and I acknowledge the debt I owe for their support.

At the end of the day, the errors and deficiencies remain my own. The support of the others has been invaluable – not least the patient encouragement of my colleagues at E.A. We are united in the common belief that issues of truth are of paramount importance to the future well-being of the church. If we lose this battle for genuine basics, our future looks bleak.

Clive Calver
London,
January 1995

1
Where Truth and Injustice Meet

In this opening chapter we consider the ways in which the idea of truth has been abused and distorted – and what the results have been. We then examine the Christian conviction that truth can only be found in God.

Where Truth and Injustice Meet

Father: 'I want an explanation and I want the truth.'
Son: 'Make up your mind, Dad, you can't have both.'

Anon

Cancelled!

I read the word with mounting horror and amazement. The brief letter said it all. Graham Kendrick and I were to have taken our team, 'In the Name of Jesus', to conduct a mission in a small Sussex town. Now the church had withdrawn the invitation – and at very short notice.

The reason confronted me in black and white. The accusation was simple: 'Because you have white witches in your meetings.' The shock to a young evangelist was overwhelming. There were many things of which I would be guilty, but how could this be one of them?

I hunted my memory banks, and recalled the relevant incident. Three years previously I had joined in a partnership mission between two churches in a Hampshire town. We had encountered a small coven of white witches and began to talk about Jesus with one of their young novices.

He was profoundly interested in the message of Jesus, but confused through his preliminary skirmishes with witchcraft. One evening some of the leaders of the visiting church team agreed to meet him, along with two of the leaders of the coven. They arranged to talk in an upstairs room of the church in which I was leading the meeting that night. They asked me to join them after the service and I gladly agreed.

The two witches were not even in the meeting. They just met church leaders on the premises.

I wish I could record that the novice rejected witchcraft and came to faith in Christ. Or that the two witches were left dumbstruck and convicted by the gospel. To the best of my knowledge that did not happen. The exchanges were courteous, Christian truth was shared openly and honestly, and the church members were never even aware that the private meeting took place.

One person did know. The guest preacher learned of the encounter and voiced both his distress and disapproval. The next I heard was the comment years later that, 'Clive Calver has white witches taking part in his meetings!'

While I may have been guilty of naïveté and foolishness, the truth was far removed from the allegation. The real situation was totally different from the accusation. The cancellation was a miscarriage of justice, because what was missing was any attempt to ascertain the truth.

This unfortunate incident, in microcosm, parallels similar distortions of truth on the larger stage of contemporary society. When truth is misinterpreted, misunderstood, or just ignored, then the results can be catastrophic.

The misuse of truth

A defective view of truth undergirds so many of the evils that have afflicted the modern world. It has always been possible to find a good reason for doing the wrong thing. In a society which reduces objective truth to 'shades of grey', it has always been possible for 'wrong' to masquerade as 'right' with tragic consequences. For instance (and these examples run the whole range of the human condition):

The abuse of truth is seen where:

* Violence, oppression and even terrorist activities have become uncritically accepted by many as part of the struggle for 'freedom'.   *Examples of the abuse of truth*

* Nazi belief in Aryan supremacy created the climate for Hitler's holocaust and the mass extermination of millions among the Jewish people.

* Widespread abortion 'on demand' is sanctioned on the grounds that human life is said not to actually begin until emergence from the womb, despite extensive evidence to the contrary.

* Gross abuses in the sphere of animal experimentation have often been accepted because of their ultimate 'benefit' to medical science. Equally, abuses to human property or physical violence have been legitimised in the name of animal welfare.

* Civilian populations have faced deprivation, homelessness and death through indiscriminate bombing on the grounds that a bomb cannot be programmed to be selective!

* Notions of male supremacy have been employed to legitimise the suppression of women, in family, church, and society alike.

* That trite phrase 'the end justifies the means' has been over-employed in business and professional life to sanction exploitation and the misuse of authority.

The list is seemingly endless. Yet each barbaric distortion emerges from a germ of truth which has been so abused as to defy recognition of the original.

The situation becomes even more problematic when theology is brought into the picture! Scriptural support has often been claimed for practices which others would view as totally unbiblical. Here again truth is at the mercy of interpretation.

Scripture, slavery and apartheid

One vivid illustration of this is the use of the Bible to justify racism and slavery. The observation and reporting by Ham of his father Noah's naked, drunken body (Gen 9:22) was reprehensible. Yet it scarcely justifies the persecution of his presumed descendants thousands of years later!

Slavery justified from the Bible The curse which Noah placed upon Ham's son, Canaan, was that he should be the 'lowest of slaves... to his brothers' (Gen 9:25). This was to become a convenient legitimisation for the highly profitable slave trade.

Some have argued that slavery was divinely sanctioned among the Israelites. Slaves could be taken from outside their own nation (Lev 25:44-46). Their leaders and heroes were slave owners who utilised slavery for the national good (Gen 12:5, 16; 14:14; 20:14; 24:35-36; 26:13-14; 47:15-25). Slavery could be merciful, it was preferable to death, and if it was such a vile institution, then why was it never condemned by either Jesus or the apostles? (1 Tim 6:1-6).

What the advocates of this theory chose to ignore was that neither God, nor Israel, introduced the principle of servitude. Their treatment of slaves more resembled the kind of treatment appropriate to servants, and the Hebrew word '*ebhedh*' could as easily be translated 'servant' as it is 'slave'.

Slaves in Israel Slaves in Israel were granted all humanitarian benefits. They were legally protected from oppression and possessed the same civil and religious rights as their masters (Lev 24:22; Deut 1:9-17; 23:15-16). Hebrew servitude was voluntary, a protection against poverty, and automatic freedom was offered every seven years (Ex 21:2-6; Lev 25:10).

The slave trade did not exist in Israel and this may well account for Christ's silence on the subject. As for God's attitude on the matter, while the process of law was to be upheld (as in the case of Philemon and Onesimus), injustice was against his laws. The prophets denounced it, and God employed all available means to bring his people out of slavery in Egypt, and into the Promised Land.

The development of apartheid A further illustration of the abuse of truth is provided by the evil of apartheid which has crippled the young nation of South Africa for much of its existence. This has left a legacy of hatred and mistrust which may well take generations to overcome.

The bigotry of Afrikaner convictions originated in a misinterpretation of biblical truth. The Afrikaner argued that God had set up walls of separation between nations, and insisted upon the need for racial purity. Drawing on verses like Genesis 11:7, Deuteronomy 32:8 and Acts 17:26, they determined that God had given separate existences to each nation. The mixing of races would be to deny the will and purpose of God. Racial separation was regarded as a divine decree.

Afrikaners interpreted Old Testament holiness in terms of the separation of God's people, Israel, from the heathen Canaanite peoples who surrounded them. That was true. Now the New Covenant, they reasoned, demanded separation of the Christian whites from the heathen blacks. It was argued that this was God's demand.

It was to be a short journey from separation to active oppression, for 'separate but equal' is never actually equal in practice. Even if equality could be maintained it would still be oppressive, for the only logical reason for maintaining separateness is that one race considers the other to be inferior and a potential source of contamination.

This whole attempt to argue from Scripture was flawed, for the Bible gives no grounds for the oppression of black by white. Jesus could scarcely have been identified as Anglo-Saxon or Afrikaner!

Truth is therefore important, it matters! Too much has resulted from the abuse of truth for us to neglect this vital issue.

Unfortunately the issue of truth rarely emerges in today's world. Instead we have become preoccupied with the pursuit of pleasure and self-fulfilment. Rather than attempt to ascertain what is ultimately right and wrong we have become content to engage in a voyage of self-discovery. Rarely do we search for truth beyond ourselves.

We ignore truth for the sake of experience

As a result we often passively accept ideas and beliefs that are less than true. Our hunger for experience has served to preclude a passion for the truth. Yet truth is vital. If we ignore it, the foundation of our actions and the values of society will be fatally flawed.

The significance of truth

The twentieth century has not been an easy time for truth.

The abuse of truth in the twentieth century   We live at the conclusion of the bloodiest century in human history. In Europe alone, international conflict has robbed more than a hundred million people of their lives. Propaganda, brainwashing and distortion of casualty figures all illustrate that warfare is no friend to truth.

Nazi Germany was to prove the point. The sinister mastermind of misrepresentation, Joseph Goebbels, manipulated the people by producing selective information to achieve a predetermined end. Mix this with fear and the appearance of a noble vision and you have followers who will believe a lie.

Repressive and coercive dynasties have been overthrown by violent revolution, only to be superseded by even more oppressive regimes than those they have replaced. Truth remained subservient to military authority.

Totalitarian dictatorships like those of Ceaucescu in Romania, Idi Amin in Uganda and Pol Pot in Cambodia emerged to dismiss what they regarded as mere 'decadent democracy'. Concentration camps represented their response to claims of freedom, belief, and human dignity. Stalin's pogrom labour camps witnessed sixty million deaths, martyrs sacrificed in a futile attempt to suppress or subvert the individual's commitment to truth as they perceived it. For dreams of freedom and truth stubbornly refused to die in even the most hostile environment.

Martyrs for the truth   In this dark night of history the light of truth still shines brightly. Names like Solzhenitsyn, Bonhoeffer, Mandela and Romero are examples of those who were prepared to suffer and die for the freedom they believed in. Torturers may try to twist the minds or break the bodies, but twentieth-century prison literature testifies to a determined refusal to compromise the truth.

As Michael Novak has observed, 'To obey truth is to be free, and in certain extremities nothing is more clear to the tormented mind, nothing is more vital to the survival of self-respect, nothing so important to one's sense of remaining a worthy human being – of being no one's cog, part of no one's machine, and resister to death against the kingdom of lies – nothing is so clear as to hold to truth. In fidelity to truth lies human dignity'. [M.Novak, *Awakening from Nihilism*, The Templeton Address of 1994].

Put in simplest form, 'truth matters'. From childhood onwards we insist on asking questions in our unending quest for truth.

The problem has lain with the answers we have received. Politicians, philosophers, economists and clerics have all been tried and found wanting. Frustrated in the desire to know the truth some people lapse into anarchy or indifference. For the majority the cry remains, 'will we ever know the truth?'

The hunger for truth

The human spirit is not easily crushed. Its restless hunger for reality can only be appeased by that which is true. *A sense of* Offended by 'sleaze', disgusted by hypocrisy, *moral values* humankind still retains a sense of moral values. The belief remains that there is more to life than individual well-being.

Alexander Solzhenitsyn prophetically announced in his Nobel acceptance speech of 1970 that 'one word of truth outweighs the whole world.' An advancing communism made that appear unlikely. Subsequent events in Eastern Europe were to make us the witnesses of history in the making, as the demands for political and religious freedom overturned the tyranny of the countries of the former USSR.

Truth matters. Confronted by opposition and persecution, truth still demands the liberty to exist. Its resistance to repression, torture and death indicates that nothing is more important to the survival of a sense of human self-worth.

Truth is not merely subjective. It is not something we can manufacture. Truth is far longer and deeper than any *Truth is not* individual. It is not something we can control. The *merely* failure of the great dictators of the twentieth century *subjective* gives ample testimony to that fact. Truth needs to control us, and the service of truth is no bondage, but the ultimate key to human liberty.

Truth matters. Within each individual burns a restless inquiry for something beyond ourselves. We retain a sense of the infinite,

A sense that we are not alone a deep-rooted conviction that we are not alone in the universe. This recognition of truth beyond ourselves has, for many, been the first stage in their journey back towards the God who loves them.

The Christian conviction is that truth resides in God himself. When Jesus boldly announced that he was 'the way and the truth and the life' (Jn 14:6) he personalised the truth of the Father in the Son, through the Holy Spirit. In this statement he confirmed that truth comes from God and can be known and recognised in everyday life.

This truth is no mere abstract idealism just to be believed; it is also to be practised. Christian doctrine and practice are contained in the profound statement, that as disciples of Jesus, 'you will know the truth, and the truth will set you free' (Jn 8:32).

Truth is located in Jesus For Christians, truth is located in Jesus, and he has freely disclosed the truth of his person in his word. He confidently affirmed that 'your word is truth' (Jn 17:17). An immortal God is revealed by an infallible word, and when the Bible speaks, Christians believe it possesses an authority that is not human but divine. When Christians speak of truth they mean what God has disclosed in Scripture, and that this revelation is irrefutable.

I believe that Scripture is truth, and can always be trusted. All that follows flows from the conviction that 'All Scripture is God-breathed and is useful for teaching, rebuking, correcting and training in righteousness' (2 Tim 3:16). The Bible 'never had its origin in the will of man, but men spoke from God as they were carried along by the Holy Spirit' (2 Pet 1:21). Christianity does not claim to be one theory among many, but to be *the* truth. Because it meets our deepest needs it does not enslave us but releases us to live in the way for which humankind was always intended. We are set free to *be* truth in a hostile and deceptive world. To carry the truth to all who will hear it. To oppose injustice in all its forms. To act as conveyors of divine 'salt and light'.

As Francis Schaeffer observed to the Berlin Congress on Evangelism in 1966:

Historic Christianity rests upon truth – not truth as an

abstract concept, nor even what twentieth-century man regards as 'religious' truth; but objective truth... Historic Christianity rests upon the truth of what today is called 'brute facts' and not just upon an unknown experience of men in past ages... Behind the truth of such history is the great truth that the personal, infinite God is objectively 'there'. He actually exists, and Christ's redemptive and finished work actually took place at a point of time in real space-time history. Historic Christianity rests upon the truth of these things in absolute antithesis to their not being true. (F.A.Schaeffer, 'The Practice of Truth' in *One Race, One Gospel, One Task* [Worldwide Publications: Minneapolis, 1967]).

God is truly 'there'

The days when Christians could turn aside and look the other way are long gone. We live in a society whose distorted view of truth has undermined the whole foundation of the gospel we proclaim. If we neglect the truth, or still worse ignore it, then we will have sacrificed the Judaeo-Christian heritage of which we boast so much.

It has become too easy for truth to be abused. We have lost a proper sense of reverence for the truth. Too often it is lowered to the level of that which can be practically attained or achieved, rather than the heights to which we must aspire.

It is easy to limit the truth

The great compromise of truth has been to reduce it to 'the art of the possible'. The reversal of this situation can only come when we elevate our understanding of truth from the level of the human imagination to see truth as residing in the heart of God himself.

Modern society has conceived of God as different from truth, remote and alien to this world. He is seen as permanently unavailable, no longer 'at home'. Meanwhile pleasure-seeking, freedom-loving people found 'God' a symbol of restriction, and 'truth' the flagship of liberty. The two were rarely viewed as travelling together.

Truth at the heart of God

A freethinking society has adopted a whole variety of differing views. Little agreement has emerged among conflicting ideologies which have all claimed to replace God.

The result has been confusion. Uncertainty prevails. Truth is reduced to what we feel like rather than something that is absolute. Only under pressure does a passion for truth re-emerge. 'In the twentieth century, prison and torture chambers have been better places to encounter God than universities'. (M.Novak, *op cit.*)

Living the Truth

The lack of clarity about truth creates a moral as well as a philosophical vacuum. For truth affects what we do as well as who we are. The Christian gospel insists that truth can only be located and encountered in God. That confident conviction has to be sensitively announced to society and applied to its actions.

We need determination to maintain the truth as Jesus revealed it to his disciples, and to listeners among the first century crowds. Not in a spirit of bigotry and arrogance, but of caring concern. Truth has to be demonstrated to be true by the actions, activities and lifestyle of those who proclaim it in words.

Jesus and truth   It is that pattern which was so vividly displayed in the life of Jesus. He showed compassion, but declared reality. He never ignored truth, or neglected it. He *was* the truth, and always revealed that fact. In Christ truth and experience were perfectly consistent together. Grace and truth were uniquely combined in him.

When confronted with falsehood, uncertainty and injustice, we must copy his example and clearly present the truth. We can never be guilty of compromise or misdirected tolerance when faced with injustice and denial of God's commands for his created world.

Truth is always uncomfortable. It is disturbing and costly. To stand for truth will sometimes involve sacrifice, but then Jesus has never allowed his people the luxury of such an 'easy option'. He has not left us here to be passengers carried along by the culture and ideology of the society in which we live. Instead we are to act as agents of his transforming power. We are here to introduce the principles of Christ's alternative kingdom into a world which is destroying itself by ignorance of the truth.

Beginning with Me!

Our starting-point must always be with ourselves. It is as we root out every perversion and violation of truth which we have tolerated in our own Christian community, that we earn the privilege of declaring truth to others. Christians, like others, have been guilty of malicious gossip, racist attitudes, fostering our own self- interest or isolating ourselves from society. We need to repent first. Only when we demonstrate truth in our lives can we adequately reveal its message to others.

That truth will not be restricted to the bald announcement of a moral code. It will be no mere Christian version of a 'back to basics' course. Instead we will declare a *person* – this Jesus who alone can give people knowledge of God's truth and the strength to live in a manner consistent with that message.

Truth is not just a challenge to others – it is first of all a challenge to ourselves! For Jesus wants us to live by the truth knowing that it can never be finally repressed or silenced.

For the committed Christian, truth matters. Yet to an increasing degree truth is also coming to matter more to those *An increasing* who exist at the heart of secular society. A developing *awareness of* awareness that sixties society cut itself free from the *the need for* moorings of a fixed concept of truth has resulted in the *truth* desire to recover some of that which we have lost.

Recently I was part of an hour long radio debate, chaired by Simon Bates. The other participants were a Conservative MP and the Editorial Director of the Mirror Group of newspapers. I had feared that there would be little common ground. However, as we ranged across subjects as diverse as the financial integrity of MPs, alleged injustice in press reporting, the conflict of commercial interests, and the public interest, we discovered a shared concern to encourage moral standards. The key was a desire for truth. Although we might interpret truth in different ways, we each acknowledged its importance to the whole debate.

Truth matters. We cannot neglect or subordinate it to our own interests. Truth must be released in order to be the litmus paper for our individual experience and the guardian of our public morality. Truth is not redundant in the twentieth century. We lose it at our peril.

2

The Whole Truth?

The Christian faith claims that Jesus was God. In this chapter we look at varying beliefs about Jesus: Did he exist? Was he a prophet, a trickster or hypnotist? Alternatively, what evidence is there for his humanity and divinity? Did he really rise from the dead?

The Whole Truth?

*'I thirst for truth, but shall not reach it till I
reach the source'.*

Robert Browning

We all love stories about our heroes. The value that we place
upon the achievements of a historical figure can sometimes
lead to our creating a 'stained-glass window' saint out of a
mortal being. We manufacture myths to reinforce our mental
image of those whose memory we value. In this sense respect can
be blind.

It has been alleged by less than critical admirers of George
Washington that, 'he never told a lie'. That must rank as a piece
of extravagant flattery when applied to a military leader and
politician. It does, however, point to his desire for personal
integrity and the way in which he despised falsehood.

In whatever way this myth originated, it is never something he
would have claimed for himself. Deceit, half-truths and
downright lies are common to the whole of humankind. Wise
people acknowledge their weakness in this respect, *with just one
notable exception.*

Jesus of Nazareth went much further than the most avid

29

admirers of George Washington. He continually claimed for himself that he was speaking the truth in what he said. The simple phrase, 'I tell you the truth' occurs more than seventy times in the gospel records. He kept on insisting that he came into the world in order to testify to the truth (Jn 18:37).

His claim exceeded that of avoiding deceit. He announced that *Jesus as the truth* he was declaring truth which emanated from God himself (Jn 3:11), because truth was given by God to the world through Jesus Christ (Jn 1:17). He announced truth which was confirmed by God. He did not just speak truth, he was the truth (Jn 14:6).

His extravagant claim was that he revealed truth to the world and therefore illuminated the darkness of human ignorance (Lk 2:32; Jn 1:5, 8:12, 9:5). This daring assertion won him few friends among the religious leaders, but none of them were able to successfully contradict him. The average Jewish listener in the crowd was absolutely delighted.

The boldness of Jesus took people by surprise. His announcement that he was the truth meant that his opponents were liars. His statements contradicted the teaching of the religious leaders of his day. His claims contravened the idealised portrait they had of a coming Messiah who would overthrow the Romans. It might be intended to illuminate their blackness, but they had become used to living in the dark.

Ultimately Jesus was emphasising that truth is not merely the absence of lies but the actual revelation of the mind of God himself. It is a positive, not negative, concept. Nor is it a mere abstract ideal. Truth exists in God, and God has arrived in Christ as an identifiable human being. Truth could now be inspected.

True or false?

Jesus of Nazareth stands head and shoulders above all human leaders and the heroes of history.

Born in an obscure Palestinian town, the legitimacy of his birth has been questioned, and yet his influence has been felt for two thousand years. More books, songs, films, poems, plays and pictures have been produced about him than any other religious or secular leader in history.

He never raised an army, yet millions have died for their commitment to his name. So much respect has been given to him that he has been termed 'the man who cut history in half'. Indeed, for centuries, time was divided into BC and AD in recognition of his impact.

But did Jesus actually exist? This may sound a strange question, but it is one that has been asked. Despite the impact of Jesus on the people of his day, and throughout subsequent human history, there are those who doubt that he was a real person. Some have concluded that he was a figment of the imagination *Was Jesus a* of people infatuated by a dream of a true Messiah. In *real person?* other words, the person of Jesus was no more than a cunning invention of the early church.

This view was espoused by twentieth-century Communist propaganda. It suggested that the idea of a Jesus figure was *A myth?* produced in the second century AD to explain the rise of an early proletarian movement. One twentieth-century Russian encyclopedia described Jesus as 'the mythological founder of Christianity.'

The same idea was advocated by the French scholar, Paul Louis Couchard. During the 1920s and 1930s he suggested that the personality of Jesus was no more than a clever forgery. He claimed that Jesus may have been no more than 'an ingenious *A compilation* construction made up of prophetic oracles foretelling *of prophecies?* the future Messiah'. (Francois Amiot, Amedee Brunot, Jean Danielou and Henri Daniel-Rops, *The Sources for the Life of Christ* [Hawthorn Books: New York, 1962]).

In 1970 an oriental studies specialist at Manchester University, Dr John Allegro, gained a great deal of publicity through his book, *The Sacred Mushroom and the Cross*. In it he asserted that Christianity began as a secret cult of a sacred *Code for a* mushroom. Jesus was the code name for the use of a *hallucinogenic* hallucinogenic drug. The New Testament writers *drug?* became members of an ancient fertility cult. Allegro alleged that they concealed their secrets in the gospel records which amounted to an elaborate cryptogram.

This outlandish theory created quite a stir in the popular press, but the total absence of evidence has failed to generate much support from other scholars.

During the 1970s and 1980s a professor at London University, G. A. Wells, grandson of the writer H. G. Wells, hit the headlines.

Why did Paul know so little about Jesus' earthly life? He became notorious for his theories that while the Apostle Paul was a historical figure, Jesus was not. Paul appears to be ignorant of any details of Jesus' earthly life, so Wells concludes that Jesus was no more than a product of his imagination.

Wells argued that 'recent work from critical theologians themselves provides a basis for taking more seriously the hypothesis that Christianity did not begin with a Jesus who lived on earth' (G. A. Wells, *The Historical Evidence for Jesus* [Prometheus: Buffalo, 1982]). When I had to debate with Professor Wells at the Cambridge Union in 1989, I discovered that his main argument lay in the fact that the historians of the first generations of the Christian era had little to say about the life of Jesus.

This should come as no surprise to us! Dr R. T. France has pointed out that,

> From the point of view of Roman history in the first century, Jesus was a nobody. A man of no social standing, who achieved brief local notice in a remote and little loved province as a preacher and miracle-worker, and who was duly executed by order of a minor provincial governor, could hardly be expected to achieve mention in the Roman headlines. (R. T. France, *The Evidence for Jesus* [Hodder and Stoughton: London, 1986]).

In fact few authors of the time would have been interested in what they would assume was no more than a Jewish, religious rabble-rouser. Jesus was far from the only cause of religious and political disturbances. Wells' argument is weak, it has gained little theological acceptance, and his academic background is as a Professor of German, not theology!

The real evidence points in the opposite direction to that taken by the sceptics. Josephus, a renegade Jew, writing in the latter part of the first century AD, twice mentions Jesus by name. He first refers to 'James, the brother of Jesus the so-called Messiah.' He then makes a longer reference to Jesus.

In the *Testimonium Flavianium*, Josephus states,

About this time there lived Jesus, a wise man, if indeed one ought to call him a man. For he was one who wrought surprising facts and was a teacher of such people as accepted the truth gladly. He won over many Jews and many of the Greeks. He was the Messiah.

Evidence in support of Jesus' existence

When Pilate, upon hearing him accused by men of the highest standing amongst us, had condemned him to be crucified, those who had in the first place come to love him did not give up their affection for him.

On the third day he appeared to them restored to life, for the prophets of God had prophesied these and countless other marvellous things about him, and he has still to this day not disappeared. (Josephus, *Antiquities* 18:63-64).

Returning to Professor Wells – he suggests that this reference to Jesus was inserted by the Church. This is unlikely; the style is that of Josephus, and few Christians would dare to call Jesus the 'so-called Messiah' (as quoted on page 32). Others suggest that because this extract is an astonishing testimony to the Christian understanding of who Jesus really was, some Christian insertions might have taken place.

Even if some changes have been made, it still gives positive evidence of the existence of Jesus from an author who, living much of his life in Palestine, would possess a relatively contemporary understanding of what was believed about Jesus.

Jewish literature two centuries after Jesus gives little historical information about him, other than the implication that he certainly existed. In attacking Jesus, the Jewish rabbis were dealing with someone whose very name they could not bear to mention. Instead they often used very obscure quotations: 'On Passover Eve they hanged Yeshu,' and 'Jesus the Nazarene practised magic,' give the general flavour of excerpts drawn from the Babylonian Talmud.

Jewish anti-Christian attacks in the second century AD indicate a belief that he was a human born as the result of adultery of a Jewish girl, Mary, with a Roman soldier, Panthera. Jesus Ben Panthera is occasionally referred to in first-century stories as the originator of a dangerous heresy.

When one adds the mass of material from early heretics, deviant Christian groups, gnostic sects, and the writings of the early Church fathers, there remains little doubt as to the existence of Jesus.

The clinching factor is probably the testimony of two early second-century Roman historians.

Evidence from two Roman historians

Suetonius, writing about AD 120, referred to the expulsion of Jews from Rome. This, he recorded, took place 'at the instigation of Chrestus' and while Claudius was Emperor (AD 41-54). Many see 'Chrestus' as a variant spelling of Christ. Even if Suetonius was mistaken in believing that Jesus was still alive and causing trouble, it indicates his belief that a Jesus existed who led a band of dissident Jews.

Tacitus, writing between AD 115 and 117, went further, and mentioned Christ by name. He also wrote of early Christian origins in Judea and the execution of Christ under the instructions of the Roman governor, Pontius Pilate. Nearly two thousand years after they were written these words illustrate contemporary secular opinion about Jesus and his followers.

> To dispel the rumour, Nero substituted as culprits, and treated with the most extreme punishments, some people, popularly known as Christians, whose disgraceful activities were notorious. The originator of that name, Christus, had been executed when Tiberius was emperor by order of the procurator Pontius Pilate. But the deadly cult, though checked for a time, was now breaking out again not only in Judea, the birthplace of this evil, but even throughout Rome, (Tacitus, *Annals* XV, 44).

Added together these early testimonies provide clear evidence for the reality of Jesus. No-one appears to have disputed his existence. No early opponent of Christianity ever accused the church of having invented Jesus. These fanciful accusations only emerge in the twentieth century!

Who is this Jesus?

If Jesus was a genuine historical figure, then what kind of person was he? What is the truth about Jesus of Nazareth?

This question has echoed down the centuries since the day that Jesus first asked his disciples, Who do you say I am?' (Mk 8:27). At that time people were as confused and divided as they are today.

Some saw Jesus as a good man (Mk 10:17; Jn 7:12). Followers of Islam and a variety of other faiths still concur in that judgement. Jesus is recognised and respected as one of a special few, but not unique.

Others saw him as the reincarnation or successor of the past spiritual heroes (Mt 14:2; 16:14; Lk 9:19).

Many in the twentieth century would simply consider him to have been someone who would stand out in the crowd, but little more.

Religious leaders viewed him as a demonised deceiver who had not come from God (Jn 9:16). There are still those who see Jesus as a fraud, introducing deception rather than truth.

The majority view was that Jesus was a prophet, one of those who brought the message of God to humankind (Mt 16:14; Mk 8:28; Lk 7:16). This remains a popular view today. Jesus' teaching is respected and his moral stance applauded. However, appreciation of the good things he said falls far short of worship of who he claimed to be.

Pontius Pilate enquired if Jesus was King of the Jews (Mt 27:11; Mk 15:2; Lk 23:3; Jn 18:33). There are still people today who want to assign Jesus a quasi-political role, making him a leader of oppressed peoples.

Gradually those who were closest to Jesus began to recognise that he was someone very special (Jn 6:69). Finally it was Simon Peter who articulated their growing conviction, 'You are the Christ, the Son of the living God' (Mt 16:16). Subsequently the disciples boldly proclaimed this statement as the truth about God (Acts 2:31-36). The church recognised that this conviction of Jesus as the Son of God represented the very heart of their faith (1 Jn 5:5). And today nearly one third of the world's population chooses to agree with this statement.

For many of his contemporaries his identity remained uncertain. Astonished by his actions and amazed at the words of a carpenter's son, people wondered who on earth he could be, (Mt 13:54; Mk 7:37; Lk 4:22). There are still vast numbers of people who, even if they are prepared to consider the gospel accounts seriously, still remain confused and undecided. We continue to be divided about Jesus (Jn 7:40-43). Wanting to believe, but unsure where such conviction will take us, we ask with Saul of Tarsus, 'Who are you, *Lord*?' (Acts 9:5 – emphasis mine).

His early followers would have appreciated this struggle. Bewildered at the way he controlled the winds and waves, they enquired, 'What kind of man is this?' (Mt 8:27; Mk 4:41; Lk 8:25). That question remains equally relevant today.

Modern views of Jesus

At times in the history of the church it has been common to adopt the extreme, and wrong practice of persecuting those who disagree with its teachings.

Today the opposite, but equally reprehensible practice, tends to take place. Doubt has become fashionable, and distrust of orthodox traditional opinions tends to be regarded as normal.

Jesus the trickster? Consequently some fantastic ideas have emerged! The author, Hugh Schonfield, regards Jesus as a trickster who arranged his own 'crucifixion' and 'resurrection'. This was in order to establish his claim to be the Messiah. In even more *The sorcerer?* extreme vein, Morton Smith views the miracles of Jesus as acts of sorcery practised by an Egyptian priest, or performer of magical rites with specific sexual overtones.

The hypnotist? Ian Wilson has suggested that Jesus employed post-hypnotic suggestion in order to prepare his disciples to hallucinate his appearances in response to pre-arranged cues like bread and wine. These would continue for a pre-determined period after his death.

The yogi? Contemporary New Age perspectives reject biblical evidence, choosing rather to regard Jesus as a guru or yogi worthy of respect as a highly-evolved spiritual being, a minister of divine energy. The Christ- consciousness he embodied related to a separate impersonal, universal and eternal being. Others can subsequently inherit this consciousness.

The misunderstood mystic? Others believe that Jesus, in his 'lost years', between the age of thirteen and thirty, visited India, Tibet and Japan. Drawing on a Tibetan document discovered at the beginning of the century, Jesus is regarded as a mystic who preached the discovery of the consciousness of God within us all. Christianity therefore becomes a misguided external form of religion which misinterpreted the teachings of Jesus.

Many theories have evolved in a variety of attempts to separate the culturally acceptable (Jesus' teaching), from the unacceptable (his divinity). These deny the truth of the resurrection story. D. H. Lawrence, the novelist, is one example of those who believe that Jesus recovered consciousness in the tomb. His imaginative story has Jesus escaping to create a new life with a priestess of Isis. Another idea from the popular authors M. Baigent, R. Leigh and H. Lincoln has Jesus' son (the Holy Blood) arriving at Marseilles and founding a secret society.

Others view Jesus more sympathetically, seeing him as a man caught up by events and swept along by the political ambitions of Judas. Popular interpretations have included the lyrics of Tim Rice and the plays of Denis Potter. The infamous *The Last Temptation of Christ* dramatised the work of Nikos Kazantzakis and presented a mentally-deranged Jesus who sinned in his own fantasies.

Few of these theories have gained much popular support, or produced any credible evidence for their hypothesis. Some have exhibited more concern for personal notoriety or financial gain than for careful scholarship. Others have attempted to produce intelligent explanations for apparently irrational circumstances, which they regard as supernatural and therefore impossible.

Either way, these views may actually reveal more about the author of the theory than about the Jesus they have attempted to portray.

A few years ago I received a telephone call from Mike Wooldridge, Religious Affairs correspondent at the BBC. His message was a simple one.

Barbara Thiering, the Australian theologian, has written a new book. In it she alleges that Jesus resuscitated himself in the tomb. Despite his massive injuries he pushed one and a quarter tons of stone away from the entrance, and made his escape. After marrying Mary Magdalene they had two children. Jesus subsequently divorced her, remarried a lady named Lydia, they had a child and finally Jesus died in the south of France.'

Mike followed this information with a simple on the record question. 'Clive Calver, General Director of the Evangelical Alliance, what's your response?' Nonplussed, I could do no more than observe that there was as much chance of Ms Thiering being right as of Elvis Presley being proved to have been female!

There is a breed of journalist, very different from Mike Wooldridge, who can employ considerable skill and intelligence in producing the latest 'shock... horror... life on Venus' story for a particularly notorious section of the tabloid press. Sometimes this genre is emulated, or even surpassed, by the latest revelations concerning the 'true story' of Jesus Christ.

Needless to say these remain distinctly minority views. As the Roman Catholic theologian, Dr Hans Küng has affirmed: 'None of the great founders of religions lived in so restricted an area. None lived for such a terribly short time. None died so young. And yet how great his influence has been ... numerically Christianity is well ahead of all world religions.'

Perhaps the general estimation of Jesus has best been summarised in an anonymous comment from someone who reviewed the life of Jesus at its face value – a comment that would be echoed by millions of people around the world today.

Here is a young man who was born in an obscure village, the child of a peasant woman. He worked in a carpenter's shop until he was thirty, and then for three years he was an itinerant preacher. He never wrote a book. He never held an office ... Nineteen centuries have passed, and today he is the central figure of all the human race. All the armies that ever marched, all the navies that ever sailed, all the parliaments that ever sat, all the kings that ever reigned, have not affected human history as has that one solitary life.

Will the real Jesus...?

The good news is that we have an alternative to the plethora of current theories. Belief offers an equally incredible scenario, but one that draws its supporting evidence from contemporary eyewitnesses. *The Christian view of Jesus*

The conviction of the gospel writers is that Jesus lived and died as one who was a perfect human being. Born after a full-term pregnancy Jesus grew to manhood and maturity (Mt 1:25; 2:1; Lk 2:7, 40). Capable of hunger and thirst, he ate and drank as others do (Mt 21:18; Lk 4:2; 7:34-36; 14:1; 15:2, 24:41-43; Jn 19:28). He was limited by *A real human being* time and space and he travelled by everyday means (Lk 8:1; Jn 4:4). He showed normal thought processes by asking questions (Mk 9:21; Lk 2:46-47). Jesus became tired and was vulnerable to normal human processes – even death (Jn 4:6f. 19:33). He did not know everything, for example the date of the Day of Judgement (Mk 13:32), but was dependent on his Father for his extraordinary knowledge (Jn 5:19-20).

One friend caused real consternation at an evangelical conference when he suggested that the best way to understand how human Jesus was lay in recognising that he would have had to visit the toilet on a regular basis. His attempt to be controversial was highly successful as his listeners were horrified at the thought!

The humanity of Jesus was exemplified in the naturalness of his emotions. He grieved over the death of a relation (Mt 14:12), and could weep in both sympathy and disappointment (Mk 14:33-34; Lk 19:41; Jn 11:35). Jesus expressed compassion (Mt 9:36; 15:32; Mk 6:34; 8:2; Lk 15:20), and displayed love for his family and friends (Jn 15:15; 19:26).

Jesus knew what it was to feel personal indignities (Jn 19:23, 28) and to express a strength of moral indignation (Mk 3:5; 10:14; Lk 11:46; 19:45; Jn 2:15-16; 8:44). He had a will of his own, yet firmly placed his trust in his Father (Mt 10:29; 26:39; Lk 22:42; Jn 17:1-10).

In one way Jesus was different. Nobody ever accused him of sin, except the apparent blasphemy of claiming to be God, either during his ministry, or at his trial (Jn 8:46; Lk 23:4, 14, 22). The truth of God became human, and was tempted as we are, but alone lived in the manner for which we were originally designed.

The pages of Scripture reveal Jesus as an incomparable man! He possessed all the essentials of human nature in exactly the same way as God had created man in the beginning. If he was just a man there would be little problem. Yet the Bible declares that one day we will discover that Jesus is still a man. Having been raised from death, Jesus still possesses that virgin-born, crucified, buried, resurrected and now glorified body. In his Ascension he has taken manhood into the Godhead. The ascended and glorified Christ still retains his human nature. It is as a man that he intercedes for us in heaven (Rom 8:34) and as a man that he sits upon the throne.

The great wonder of the Incarnation is not just that God became man – and God died as a man – for humankind, but that God remains as a man in his glory – the Incarnation could not be reversed. Jesus is still a man (1 Tim 2:5).

The real stumbling-block with the Christian faith lies in its unequivocal claim that this is only half the story. For Christianity claims to be a unique faith unparalleled by other religions. The foundation stone of this claim lies in the affirmation that the human founder of the faith was also himself divine.

The man who is God

This staggering claim represents the heartbeat of Christianity.

Really man and really God The Apostle Paul affirmed that Jesus was God (Rom 9:5; Tit 2:13). He was joined in this claim by Peter and John (Jn 1:1-2, 18; 2 Pet 1:1), and the author of the epistle to the Hebrews (Heb 1:8). Each was unanimous in adding their voice to that of Thomas who exclaimed, 'My Lord and my God' (Jn 20:28).

From the special circumstances surrounding his birth through to his Resurrection, Jesus displayed characteristics that could not, taken together, be defined in terms of humanity alone.

The miracles of healing bore unique witness to the power and authority of Jesus. He freely forgave sins (Mk 2:5-10; Lk 7:48). Jesus demonstrated his supremacy over both evil spirits and the forces of nature (Mt 8:27-29; Mk 1:24-27; Lk 4:41).

All those who accept the truth and authority of the Bible are left in no doubt that Jesus is God. Seven clear signs in Scripture confirm the deity of Jesus.

* Prayer and worship are addressed to him (Mt 28:17; Acts 7:59f; 9:13f; Rom 9:5; Rev 5:12).

* He is the Saviour of sinners (Jn 3:17; Acts 4:12; 5:31; 15:11; Gal 1:4; Eph 5:25).

* Jesus sent his disciples to bear witness to him in exactly the same way as his Father had (Is 43:10; Acts 1:8).

* The glory of God is revealed in Jesus (1 Cor 2:8; 2 Cor 4:4; Heb 1:3; Jas 2:1).

* Jesus is the key to creation. He brought all things into being, and sustains everything in existence (Jn 1:1-3; Heb 1:3). He is leading the created universe to its destiny and will inaugurate the new creation (Rom 11:36; Col 1:16; 3:10; Phil 3:20; 2 Pet 3; Rev 21 - 22).

* Divine names were given to Jesus (Mt 2:15; 3:17; 14:33; Mk 1:11; 12:6; Jn 11:27). God the Father himself singled out Jesus as his Son and indicated his delight in him (Mt 3:17; 17:5).

* Jesus will return to earth as Judge and King (Mt 25:31-46; Jn 5:22, 27, 30; 17:5, 24).

The first Christians clearly believed that Jesus was God, and were prepared to die confident in that conviction. They saw Jesus as the author of salvation and fulfilment of prophecy (Acts 3:18, 25-26; 4:11; 10:43), and rejoiced that he now was the ascended Lord sharing with his Father in the government of the world (Acts 5:31; 10:36, 42).

When the church called Jesus 'Lord', it used a word which the Greek version of the Jewish scriptures (the Septuagint) uses to translate God's holy name, 'Yahweh'. The words 'Lord' and 'Yahweh' were the same. Today we are so familiar with the word 'Lord' that we fail to grasp its significance in the time of Jesus.

Many times when the early Christians called Jesus 'Lord' it had a deep significance (1 Cor 16:22; Rev 22:20). The Ptolemies of Egypt and the Roman Emperors only allowed this phrase to be used because they fostered the cult of themselves as gods.

Archaeological discoveries at Oxyrhyncus place this matter beyond doubt. So when the New Testament writers spoke of Jesus as Lord, there can be no doubt that they meant it to be understood that he was God.

The Resurrection of Jesus

Nowhere was this more clearly demonstrated than in the

Resurrection of Jesus. Only one who was God himself could rise from the dead and ascend to his Father. This truth was vital to the church and has survived innumerable attacks upon it (2 Cor 4:14).

There have been many theories devised to discount the Resurrection, but none has finally succeeded in proving the case. Without examining all the evidence it is worth emphasising that the tomb was empty – and no-one to date has produced the body. Geza Vermes, the Jewish scholar, has had to admit: '[There is] one disconcerting fact; namely that the women who set out to pay their last respects to Jesus found not a body but an empty tomb.'

Evidence for the Resurrection
As we have seen earlier, D. H. Lawrence and others have suggested that Jesus may have later recovered. But could someone who had been beaten, crucified, pierced with a spear and left overnight in a cold tomb to bleed, really survive and roll away a huge stone from the entrance?

One has to ask about the Roman guard placed outside the tomb. If soldiers lost a living prisoner they had to serve his sentence instead. For losing an executed felon the penalty would be death. Furthermore, how could someone so well known, in a small country, just vanish off the face of the earth?

In 1945 the Israeli archaeologist Professor Sukenik discovered a sealed tomb outside Jerusalem. It contained five bone caskets, and a coin that confirmed the date the tomb was sealed at around AD 50. On one of the caskets was scratched the inscription: 'Jesus, let him arise,' and 'Jesus, help'. They clearly point to the belief of those who had died in a Lord of life who can raise the dead.

As Michael Green has observed:

> It would be difficult to imagine any archaeological finds which could more clearly illustrate the burning faith of the early church in the Jesus whom many of them had known personally as a historic figure walking the streets of Palestine a few years previously (M. Green, *Runaway World* [IVP: London, 1969]).

No arguments can finally prove or disprove the truth of the Resurrection. The weight of historical evidence is, however, extraordinarily high, and few objective investigations have attempted to disprove it.

Throughout the centuries the church has known the risen Christ, and confidently anticipated his return. The cry 'Maranatha', 'Come O Lord', still echoes today – because we are certain that he will be back!

The truth of God

The significance of Jesus is both immense and incomparable. The American essayist Ralph Waldo Emerson once commented, 'The name of Jesus is not so much written, as ploughed into the history of the world'.

If Jesus had simply been born of human parents, lived as a moral instructor, and then retired to the grave he would be almost universally regarded as one of the greatest ethical teachers of all time.

The difficulty about Jesus does not lie in what he taught about others, but in the things that he clearly said about himself. The claims that he made about his own identity demand that we conclude him to be either a liar or God himself.

The only alternative is to question his sanity. The Oxford scholar C.S. Lewis explained that:

> A man who was merely a man and said the sort of *Moral teacher,* things Jesus said would not be a great moral *madman or* teacher. He would either be a lunatic – on a level *God?* with the man who says he is a poached egg – or else he would be the devil of hell. You must make your choice. Either this man was, and is, the Son of God: or else a madman or something worse (C. S. Lewis, *Mere Christianity* [Fontana: London, 1952]).

We must face up to serious questions before we assume that Jesus was either the victim of self-delusion or the perpetrator of a massive hoax on humankind.

Could the founder of a profoundly moral faith, majoring on truth, be no more than a fraud? Would a fraud who was sane be prepared to suffer crucifixion for something he knew to be a lie?

If Jesus were actually mad, then how could he have lived and acted in the extremely sane way that he did?

The confident assertion of Jesus was that he was the living embodiment of the truth of God. He had no doubt about who he was, and that to be the truth he could be no less than God himself.

When Simon Peter announced that Jesus was the Christ, Jesus confirmed that this information could only have come from his Father (Mt 16:17). God's truth was not a principle, but a person, one who bore the name Jesus.

I once had to chair a debate at the Royal Albert Hall between Moslems and Christians. The issue was whether Mohammed or Jesus was the true messenger of God. One of the frustrations of that type of role is that as Chairman one has to keep warring factions apart from each other. The Chairman is not allowed to make a contribution to the debate.

Jesus' own claim to be God   Imagine my frustration when one of the Christians was challenged to show where Jesus had himself claimed to be the Son of God. The challenge was avoided! Yet time and again Jesus took the holy name for God, used in the Old Testament, and applied it to himself.

He confidently announced that he was truly the great 'I am'. In Greek the words *ego eimi,* mean 'I, I am,' but are simply translated into English as 'I Am'. He employed it to describe himself (Jn 6:48; 10:7, 11; 11:25; 14:6; 15:1). He used it to Jewish soldiers when they came to arrest him in the Garden, and they fell back at the enormity of his apparent blasphemy (Jn 18:5-6).

Our lack of confidence in proclaiming the reality of the uniqueness and divinity of Jesus is little short of scandalous. He had no such qualms. He told the Jewish High Priest who he was (Mk 14:61-62). He accepted the judgement of others as to his divinity (Mt 27:40, 43). Jesus used the intimate expression *Abba,* 'Daddy', when talking to his Father and this was unprecedented within Judaism.

Jesus knew that he existed before his birth at Bethlehem (Jn 1:1-3, 27-30; 16:26-28; 17:1-5; Lk 12:49-51). He even boldly affirmed that he predated Abraham (Jn 8:58) in a further use of *ego eimi* to state who *he* is.

Jesus knew that he was uniquely God's truth. Over the centuries the church has accepted this as fact. In recent years we have tried to water it down to make our message palatable to modern ears. By so doing we only succeed in denying the truth he came to introduce.

To return to C. S. Lewis:

> You can shut him up for a fool, you can spit at him and kill him as a demon; or you can fall at his feet and call him Lord and God. But let us not come with any patronising nonsense about his being a great human teacher. He has not left that open to us. He did not intend to (C. S. Lewis *op cit*).

3
Objection, My Lord!

This chapter considers the challenges posed to Christian truth by the rise of science; the effects of secularisation and technological development, modern psychology and biblical scholarship.

Objection, My Lord!

Once to every man and nation
Comes the moment to decide,
In the strife of Truth with Falsehood,
For the good or evil side.

James Russell Lowell.

The Son of God was on trial for his life, his silence more eloquent than words could ever have been. One man was in an awful quandary. Persuaded of the innocence of his prisoner, *The quandary* a weak-willed politician was caught between the *facing Pontius* vehemence of the Jewish religious leaders and his own *Pilate* sense of justice. His response to this dilemma would secure him an unenviable place in history.

Had it not been for this encounter with an itinerant Jewish religious teacher, Pontius Pilate would now be long-forgotten. It is easy to sympathise with him. A riot in Jerusalem would have capped a career distinguished only by a series of spectacular blunders in which he continually offended Jewish religious sensitivities. Imperial Rome would not be likely to tolerate its inept servant for much longer. Confronted by an angry mob, Pilate was always likely to choose the easy way out. Knowing

49

that he dare not further incur the wrath of the Jews, he protested that Jesus was not guilty. He then released a murderer and condemned an innocent man to death.

Forever immortalised as the Governor who sentenced Jesus to crucifixion, three snapshots of Pilate live on. He is remembered as washing his hands to avoid an unpleasant decision; he is renowned for the infamy of surrendering to the demands of the mob; and for asking Jesus, 'What is truth?' (Jn 18:38), but turning away before an answer could be given.

That single question has reverberated along the passages of history. Probably no single period of time has offered less of a reply than the twentieth century. Pilate's question 'What is truth?' remains, and our silence is deafening.

The issue of truth rarely emerges into clear focus today. The subjectivism of twentieth-century society does not readily lend itself to discussions of objective truth. Our common emphasis on material possessions and personal experience creates an obsession with 'my way' at the expense of any consideration of '*the* way'.

This neglect has far-reaching consequences. We are in grave danger of sacrificing something of very great value. The dictionary *The nature of* answer to Pilate's first-century question is that truth is *truth* 'faithfulness; constancy; veracity; agreement with reality;... that which is true or according to the facts of the case; the true state of things'. (*Chambers English Dictionary* [Cambridge University Press: Cambridge, 1988]).

When viewed in this light, questions relating to the substance of truth assume a staggering importance. For the nature of truth is bound up in the way life should be lived and the existence of ultimate certainties and reality beyond ourselves.

The discovery of that which is just and right therefore constitutes the major objective of life on this planet. To know the truth is not enough. Truth is no mere cerebral matter, it is the condition of life itself. It is not there to be merely understood or spoken, but to be practised.

Living with a hunger for truth will be the source of inestimable benefits. Truth provides:

* A basis for relationships and a firm foundation for family life.

The benefits * A basis for justice and its operation within the local *of truth* community and wider society.

* A basis for consistent ethical and moral standards.
* A basis for a proper direction, vision, plans and progress for life.
* A basis for personal and collective honesty and integrity.

Such truth is far from being mundane or boring. It is no mere abstraction, or collection of unattainable ideals. For truth can be liberating, edifying, inspiring and motivating. It is therefore instructive and corrective, and provides the basis for individual and collective improvement.

The pursuit of truth is important at a practical level, as it ensures a proper foundation for scientific and technological progress. At an emotional level it offers safety, certainty and security. Spiritually, the desire for truth opens up the possibility of personal conversion and a transformed life.

Truth may therefore be recognised as a source of hope. The tragedy is that a fantastically exciting matter is largely ignored by the majority of the population. This breakdown of *The effects of* interest has infected Western society with a mood of *scepticism* scepticism about truth to the point where many deny the existence of any such thing as absolute truth. 'Whose truth, yours or mine?' 'Can't trust the papers to get it right'. 'No such thing as black and white, just shades of grey'. 'Can't tell the difference between truth and lies any more'. 'It may be true for you, but not for me!'

Truth has now become largely subjective. What I believe to be right must be so. The individual has become their own self-fulfilling arbiter of truth. The elusive character of any truth that might exist beyond the boundary of my own value system has now disappeared over the horizon. The significance of 'personal relationships' alone retains the character of an absolute in much of Western society.

Past generations sang the praises of firmly-rooted concepts of truth. How can it be that we have so quickly mislaid them? Perhaps the ultimate reason lies in our rejection of faithful adherence to a belief in God, Scripture and the practice of an active Christian life. Instead we have become submerged in a welter of conflicting ideas which have replaced the dominant Christian ideas of previous generations. These were based on a commitment to the presupposition that truth existed – and could be uncovered in the person of Jesus Christ, the doctrinal teaching of the church, and in the pages of the Bible itself.

Christians have always believed that God himself is the divine repository of truth. God is truth, and truth cannot exist apart from him. If God deserted truth he would be less than God, and truth without God must always represent an unattainable ideal. It is his arch-enemy Satan who is 'the father of lies' (Jn 8:44).

The drift away from God
Ever since disobedience entered Eden's garden humankind has resisted the truth, which represented God's pattern of life for his people (Rom 1:25). Contemporary society has gone one step further. Not content with rejecting God's truth, we have 'come of age' and now deny that it even exists.

Within contemporary society this drift away from God has been reinforced by a number of significant factors. The development of science and technology, the emergence of modern psychological theories, the rise of secularism and the popularisation of liberal theology have all combined to undermine our commitment to traditional notions of truth. In some cases, as with the idea of the earth being flat, these were wrong, yet too often we have assumed that modern theories must always be correct.

The challenge of scientific discovery

We live in an age of science. Its influence penetrates the whole of contemporary society. It is honoured, trusted and frequently regarded as infallible. The scientist speaks the oracle and society announces that it is good – and it often is.

While science can never answer the 'why?' of the world around us, it does examine the 'how?' When scientist and biblical scholar collide in their views, then the Christian understanding of truth is inevitably challenged.

Modern scientific discoveries, especially in the spheres of biology, geology and physics, have challenged the truth of the biblical narrative relating to creation itself.

The nineteenth century witnessed a frightening schism between science and religion. Some scientists have claimed that biblical theories of creation are totally disproved. However, scientific theories are continually being modified or changed in the light of fresh discoveries.

Today we can draw upon the scholarship of many scientists who, while disputing the means of the formation of the universe, will affirm that it has both significance and purpose. *Do science and* Some can freely affirm their belief in a personal God. *the Christian* They maintain that to believe in the Creator who has *faith have to* revealed himself in both nature and Scripture *conflict?* involves no inherent contradiction or ultimate conflict between the two. Such views recognise that our understanding of both is incomplete and that final conclusions as to how they fit together may have to wait until we can address the author of both face to face.

It is too easy to reject the scholarly expertise of scientists merely because they are also committed Christians. The Cambridge scholar and atheist Professor Richard Dawkins, attacks Christianity and receives public acclaim, but he is an atheist. We have no more grounds for dismissing the views of Christian academics as biased than for regarding Professor Dawkins as the servant of his own presuppositions.

Much attention has recently been devoted to the work of Dr Stephen Hawking. The astrophysicist, Carl Sagan, in his introduction to Hawking's book, acclaimed it as, 'A book about God ... or perhaps about the absence of God ... The word God fills these pages ... a universe with no edge in space, no beginning or end in time, and nothing for God to do'. (S. Hawking, *A Brief History of Time* [Bantam: London, 1988]).

Yet the question of God's existence is not ruled out by *A supreme* Hawking himself. He freely admits, 'I thought I had left *being?* the question of the existence of a supreme being completely open. . . It would be perfectly consistent with all we know to say that there was a being responsible for the laws of physics' (S. Hawking, Letters to the Editor: Time and the Universe, *American Scientist,* 73 [1985]).

Professor Paul Davies, the Australian physicist, draws attention to an enormous resurgence of interest in the interface between science and religion. He comments upon the current debate:

At some finite instant in the past the universe of space, time and matter is bounded by a space-time singularity. The coming-into-being of the universe is therefore represented not only by the abrupt appearance of matter, but of space and time as well... Where did the Big Bang occur? The bang did not occur at a point in space at all. Space came into existence with the Big Bang... What happened before the Big Bang?... St. Augustine long ago proclaimed that the world was made with time and not in time, and that is precisely the modern scientific position. (P. Davies, *The Mind of God* [Simon and Schuster: New York, 1992]).

Where was the Big Bang?

While some maintain that the origin of life itself clearly remains outside the realm of scientific investigation, others point to the basic harmony between scientific theory and the Genesis order of creation. Many remain content to separate the world of faith from issues of continuing scientific discovery. They argue that while Scripture teaches religious truth, science offers its physical counterpart. The two are therefore closer to being partners than opponents.

Partners or opponents?

Clearly it is now no longer correct to claim that science denies Christianity. The biblical view of the Creator and his creation has survived an enormous assault – yet this information is largely withheld from the general public on the ground that it is not newsworthy! The quiet and cogent arguments of a battalion of Christians involved in scientific research are ignored, because they lack the sensationalism required to receive public exposure.

No longer can science and religion be regarded as having assumed 'action stations' against each other. Instead a fog of confusion exists. Many believe that clearer air lies ahead, with no irreconcilable contradiction existing between the proponents of scientific theory and the adherents of Christian faith.

Professor Donald Mackay confirmed this change of status shortly before his death. He affirmed that, 'Today the echoes of the great nineteenth century conflict have almost died away, and theologians and scientists once more pursue their callings side by side in peace.' (D. Mackay, 'Science and Christian Faith Today', in *Real Science, Real Faith* [Monarch: Eastbourne, 1991]).

The challenge of secularisation

The years since the Industrial Revolution have witnessed an amazing transformation in our society. As the process of industrialisation transformed the face of Europe so people uprooted themselves from their rural habitat and flocked into the towns and cities. Education, science, technology and the capitalistic drive to profit and efficiency provided new influences on lifestyle and belief.

Population mobility meant that people relocated themselves for reasons of employment, promotion and economic survival. This uprooting destroyed traditions of church commitment. After moving to a new community many never regained the habit of church-going. *The effects of population movement*

Where society becomes more impersonal, so Christian contact is reduced, and the smaller the percentage of church-goers tends to become. New communities lack a tradition of religious involvement. So the church loses influence, and Christian ideas and institutions are displaced from the centre of modern society and relegated to its margins. The same process has affected many other community-based activities.

Demoted from its privileged position, the church and organised religion became a major casualty. Religious views of truth and traditional concepts of right and wrong were progressively discarded as the church cast a contracting shadow upon society. The Christian claim of being relevant, and presenting standards of truth for the whole spectrum of life, became largely ignored.

The sociologist R. H. Tawney observed:

> Religion has been converted from the keystone which holds together the social edifice, into one of the departments within it, and the idea of a rule of right is replaced by economic expediency as the arbiter of policy and the criteria of conduct. (R. H. Tawney, *Religion and the Rise of Capitalism* [New American Library: New York, 1926]). *Religion replaced by economic expediency*

All truth is now viewed as needing to be securely rooted in the 'real world'. Worship, the spiritual dimension of life, and the prospect of the eternal are dismissed as esoteric concepts. Reality lies in the material here and now. The secular and spiritual have been clearly divorced from each other. Concepts of Christian truth and values can no longer be regarded as 'norms' for society – unless they can be demonstrated as working for people today.

Religious ideas of truth which challenge established practice are therefore relegated to the pages of history. Love is viewed as okay, but self-sacrifice is looked at as dangerous extremism, and today is not seen as a time for idealism. Os Guinness has commented on the devastating results of this twentieth-century drift into secularism and a dehumanised society:

The effect of secularisation   Secularisation is the acid rain of the spirit, the atmospheric cancer of the mind and the imagination. Vented into the air not only by industrial chimneys but by computer terminals, marketing techniques and management insights, it is washed down shower by shower, the deadliest destroyer of religious life the world has ever seen. (O. Guinness, *The Gravedigger File* [Hodder and Stoughton: London,1983]).

The handmaiden of this secularising process has been the development of technology. This does not mean that Christians should seek to oppose technological progress. Far from it. Yet we do need to be more aware of its implications.

Technology has made great contributions to society. Industrial growth, health care and communications have all benefited from its development. Our lives have been made easier, but step by step technology has contributed to the erosion of public awareness of the significance of Christian truth. Once society existed as a 'tribal' community in which people needed one another. Today the depersonalisation of the individual has become a fact of life. Many have now been made redundant by the microchip or the machine. Many have retreated into an independent box supported by technological appliances.

The value of the person   The notion that human beings are special, the truth that we are made in the image of God (Gen 1:27), has come to be regarded as a primitive hangover from less-civilised days. Yet deep inside the longing remains for involvement in a community where everybody knows our name. Soap operas give us a second-hand vision of the friendship that many would love to have (though without the crises presented by TV drama).

Material possessions have often replaced spiritual realities and values as the test of personal worth. Viewed in terms of self-sufficient immediacy, our world sees little need for God – or eternity. Reality is now, the future can take care of itself.

Only when that future is threatened, as by fears of global warming, does environmental concern appeal to a majority of the population. Basically we live for the here and now. Our modern world is convinced that it has come of age. God is no longer necessary, unless one wants him to be so. Medicine, agricultural method and domestic appliances have removed the need for him. The comment of a recent TV documentary was both explicit and succinct. 'We seem to have given ourselves over to technology'. (*White Heat,* BBC2, 10 October 1994).

We can freely acknowledge the benefits provided by the development of modern industry, while recognising the tendency to regard such developments as removing *Do we still need God?* the sense of need for God. The danger comes from rejecting prayer when we have the medical profession and the social services. After all, who needs God when we can care for ourselves? Yet many in the medical profession are committed Christians who freely acknowledge that medical science only goes so far in the quest to respond to human need.

Imagine being in a modern-day fishing boat on the Sea of Galilee with the other disciples. Jesus lies asleep in the boat. A storm begins. What do you do? Wake Jesus? No, you'd probably start up the engine and head for the shore. There would appear to be no need to disturb Jesus. That is a vivid picture of the response of modern humanity. The new technological advances have removed the need for God. Why pray to God for help when you can rely on an outboard motor?

Despite all this a sense of 'cosmic loneliness' still pervades the human spirit. Many people still long for spiritual realities, for someone to pray to! Christians can avoid being contemporary Luddites seeking to smash machinery, while recognising that human ingenuity can never replace the need for God. The spirit still needs its Saviour, and when human effort fails, God still remains the same Lord who provides the new materials for our progress. He alone can never be redundant.

In response to the challenge of the microchip we need to encourage a responsible and human approach towards technology. It must never be allowed to become the focus of modern idolatry, with technocrats exercising the function of high priests. Neither angel nor demon, technology is a neutral force. Its development – whether to facilitate weapons of mass destruction, to access self-designed pornography, or to add to human efficiency and welfare – will depend on the user, not merely on the hardware or software employed.

Technology has also encouraged escapism, through the use of virtual reality techniques, to insulate us from the hardship of life in the real world. Replacing actuality with fantasy may tempt the immature, but neither information technology, nor our favourite soap opera, should prevent us from encountering truth as it really is.

Technology will always bear the hallmark of the moral concept of the designer. That person is human, so technology is flawed. It can never be completely representative of truth.

For the Christian, ultimate truth resides beyond the microchip. It has to inhabit the spirit, not just the mind, and finds its origin and fulfilment in God himself. After all, he is no mere technocrat, and while technology is not dismissed by truth, it is superseded by the divine.

The challenge of modern psychology

After the 1960s, following the rebuilding of society after the Second World War, the West became increasingly preoccupied with the individual. Your growth as a person was felt to be lacking unless you had passed through an identity crisis, and engaged in a search for self-discovery! This inner quest for self-understanding then began to give way to a search for self-fulfilment through material possessions. The 'drop-out' began a distinct metamorphosis into the 'go-getter'.

Truth, self-awareness and the cult of the individual

Since the early 1980s it has become increasingly popular to engage in processes and techniques designed to foster an attitude of self-assessment. The search for personal focus and identity has urged us to discover our own self-image and engage in self-awareness. By examining our motives and actions we continue a journey towards self-discovery.

The logical conclusion of living in what has been called the 'me' generation is that everyone is urged to 'know yourself'. The result is a concept of truth which resides in the individual alone. Each of us is regarded as an independent existent self who remains basically the same, through all the changing circumstances of life.

This perception owes a distinct debt to the American psychologist, Abraham Maslow, who urged each individual to travel on a journey of self-actualisation, with the ultimate prize of personal truth in self-discovery.

Others, like B. F. Skinner, have stressed the significance of our conditioning by the environment in which we find ourselves. We therefore view ourselves as a bundle of conditioned reflexes to circumstances beyond ourselves.

The influence of unconscious forces within ourselves has been emphasised by other psychologists. Sigmund Freud concentrated on the sexual libido as a driving force, while Carl Jung concentrated on the development of the whole person through the conflict between our conscious and unconscious perceptions.

This emphasis on self-analysis owed its origins to the thinking of William James, the nineteenth-century American psychologist. His conclusion was that self-esteem depended on individual self-judgements in terms of human value. These would be influenced by the opinions of others, and be accompanied by an emotional response.

This present-day concentration on the self has left little room for the analysis of objective truth. A preoccupation with the individual precludes the possibility of collective reality. Truth cannot be universal, my truth is mine and applies to no-one else.

For the individual, can truth be universal?

Concepts of ultimate reality are therefore reduced to the level of human experience. No longer is it regarded as credible to search for truth beyond ourselves. That truth which exists is contained within the individual themselves.

Truth therefore has become a matter of personal preference, a facet of understanding prefigured by Lewis Carroll:

'Would you tell me, please, which way I ought to go from here?' asked Alice.

'That depends a good deal on where you want to get to,' said the Cat.

'I don't much care where...' said Alice.

'Then it doesn't matter which way you go,' replied the Cat.

This cold, directionless and unfriendly universe of modern thought has left people with a sense of cosmic loneliness. The individual is isolated in a universe devoid of hope. Thoughts of final destiny have been relegated to the back of people's minds. Truth is 'me' and limited to the present.

Man at the centre   In the face of these ideas the whole concept of objective truth collapses. We are the centre of our own universe, time is the extent of our experience, earth the limit of our environment, and the material the measure of our value. In the absence of truth it is not surprising that so many people today either opt out in despair, or turn inwards to an easy escapism via sport or the soap opera.

The Christian response is simple and straightforward. There is more to truth than the here and now, heaven opens a door of hope, spiritual realities beckon, and God is the centre of the universe. The heart of the gospel is that the Creator is to be worshipped, not the creature, for he is the locus of truth.

The challenge to the Bible

This message of truth and hope was clearly declared in the pages of the Bible. Yet here again the battle lines have been drawn.

Recent scholars argue that because the Bible was written by men and women it was a purely human production. Biblical writers, they suggest, were not impartial about the matters of which they wrote, and therefore display frequent natural bias. In other words, Scripture is not viewed in terms of objective fact, history or truth: it is seen as the record of events as filtered through the memory and perception of the biblical writers. They have, therefore, handed down to us the significance of the events as *they* saw them.

This point of view does not suggest that the Bible lies. It argues that the gospel writers were convinced that Jesus was the Son of God, so they simply interpreted events to give substance to their claims. We therefore have a book made up of saga, legend, myth, folklore and stories, designed to help us view things in the same way as did the early church.

Critics of the accuracy of Scripture have pointed to the selective nature of the material used. The great empires of Babylonia, Persia, Egypt, Greece and *How selective is the Bible?* Rome are only mentioned when they affect tiny, insignificant Israel and Judah. Tribal chieftains like Abraham, and local seers such as Elisha, are given chapters of text, while the great heroes of civilisation pass unmentioned. Plato, Julius Caesar, Socrates, Aristotle and Alexander the Great are not mentioned by name anywhere in the Bible.

The reality is that the Bible does not purport to be history in the normal sense of the word – but this does not affect the integrity of its factual character or historicity. The biblical writers were producing 'sacred history', the story of God's dealings with a particular people for a specific purpose. Their concern was not with the wisdom, wealth or might of the world, but with God's saving acts towards his people.

While catastrophic events were happening all around them, with empires collapsing, disasters occurring, and armies being annihilated – one great theme provides the sole focus of the biblical writers. That was the initiative and activity of a loving, all-powerful God towards a rebellious mini-nation.

> The sweep of this sacred history is magnificent. Although it omits the greatness of human civilisation which would feature prominently in any history of the world written by men, yet in principle, and from God's point of view, it tells the whole story of man from start to finish, from the beginning when 'God created the heavens and the earth' to the end when he will create 'a new heaven and a new earth' (Gen 1:1; Rev 21:1,5). (John Stott, *Understanding the Bible* [Scripture Union:London, 1984]).
>
> *Sacred history*

These accounts were therefore selective, but not fiction. They concern real events, though viewed from a divine rather than a human perspective. They do not constitute consecutive history, but truth viewed from God's standpoint.

The same problems have been raised concerning the New Testament. When contemporary church leaders and theologians question the factual accuracy of the Gospels, they are not putting forward new theories. They are simply rehearsing objections which date back to the influential philosopher/theologian Friedrich Schleiermacher, and the so-called 'Enlightenment'.

The closed-circuit universe   The eighteenth-century theory was that this world was a closed-circuit, mechanistic universe. God, if he ever existed, had set this world in motion and established natural laws to govern its operations. So the seasons, day and night, sun and moon, follow each other with monotonous regularity. God had absented himself, leaving the world to its pre-ordained pattern.

This idea precluded any possibility of God's intervening in our world. The supernatural, and any miraculous act, is therefore totally out of the question.

A modern interpretation of miracles   Critics of the Gospel records have argued that we now know better than to believe in miracles. It is maintained that these reflect the pre-scientific culture of the age in which they were written. If by 'true' we mean that they literally took place then these stories cannot represent the truth.

So the story of the feeding of the five thousand cannot be taken literally. It has been suggested that what actually happened was one boy produced his loaves and fishes, selfish consciences were pricked and all the crowd became prepared to share their hidden lunch boxes with each other.

The incident of Jesus walking on water has been similarly explained away. It is held that this was humanly impossible, and as miracles are ruled out of the question, must simply reflect the way that the disciples regarded the personality and authority of Jesus. The Gospels are not viewed as history but as 'myths'. Their historical validity is therefore irrelevant, these are merely stories told to illustrate a spiritual point. It was therefore irrelevant whether Jesus walked on water or not: it was the *real* meaning that was important. Others adopt a more popular liberalism, arguing that the disciples (quaint old fellows as they were) merely thought Jesus was walking on water because they saw him in these terms through 'eyes of faith': he could not have done this so must have been walking on stepping stones or in shallow water! How an experienced local fisherman, like Peter, knew less than the carpenter Jesus about the depth of the lake at this point has never been satisfactorily explained!

The accusation is simply levelled at the writers of the Gospels that they fabricated truth in order to vindicate the 'vested interests' of the early church. The argument is that the church invented those things which Jesus said or did which might proclaim him to be the Messiah – in which case the New Testament urgently needs to be demythologised!

The 'vested interests' of the early church

Moreover, much of the New Testament may have been taken from other sources. Scholars like Rudolf Bultmann have powerfully maintained that where anything in the teaching of Jesus might have been borrowed from elsewhere, then it simply cannot be trusted. So any parallel of a saying or event with either ancient Jewish tradition, or the beliefs of the early Church, must cast doubt on its authenticity.

We are left with only those parts of the New Testament which no-one would wish to believe about Jesus. The violent cleansing of the Temple by an angry Jesus is one of the few stories which falls into this category. This is therefore regarded as reliable, but little else is accepted as literal truth.

A few years ago a newspaper cartoon depicted a crowd of visitors being given a conducted tour of Durham Cathedral. (The then Bishop of Durham was popularly regarded as a particularly liberal scholar). One brash American demanded of their guide, 'Hey, I gather you guys don't believe in the Bible any more'. The staff member disappeared to return a moment later brandishing half a sheet of paper torn from the New Testament. He triumphantly announced to the bewildered guests, 'But this part we do believe!'

The caricature is unfair, but we do well to remember that the Bible itself rejects such selectivity. The apostle Paul reminded Timothy that, '*All* Scripture is God-breathed and is useful for teaching' (2 Tim 3:16, emphasis mine).

Faced with this barrage of objections to biblical truth, we have

How can we be sure that the Bible is trustworthy? to ask the inevitable question, 'how can I be sure?' It is important to recognise that biblical scholars are not united in their judgements. Critical opinions are constantly changing. New theories emerge and are discarded on a regular basis.

For much of the early part of this century it was relatively easy to maintain that the biblical records contained little more than a highly colourful and selective view of world events, employed by narrow religious minds to prop up their particular beliefs. The more extreme critics suggested that there was little or no evidence that biblical personalities had even existed, or that biblical events had actually occurred.

Recent scholarship suggests different conclusions Today the tide of theological scholarship is turning. More conservative scholars have employed careful and academically credible methods to draw very different conclusions from those of their more liberal counterparts.

Many archaeologists would now echo the words of William Albright in his assertion that, 'There can be no doubt that archaeology has confirmed the substantial historicity of Old Testament tradition.' Furthermore the Jewish archaeologist, Nelson Glueck, announced that, 'It may be stated categorically that no archaeological discovery has ever controverted biblical reference'.

Similarly, Professor F. F. Bruce was at pains to point out the vast number of early biblical manuscripts in comparison to other less-criticised ancient historical works. He points out:

> For Caesar's Gallic Wars (composed between 58 and 50 BC) there are several extant manuscripts, but only nine or ten are good and the oldest is some 900 years later than Caesar's day.
>
> Of 142 books of the Roman history of Livy (59 BC – AD17) only 35 survive; these are known to us from not more than 20 manuscripts of any consequence, only one of which, and that containing fragments of Books III -VI, is as old as the fourth century.
>
> Of the 14 books of the History of Tacitus (c.AD 100) only four and a half survive; of the sixteen books of his Annals, ten survive in full and two in part. The text of these extant

portions of his two great historical works depends entirely on two manuscripts, one of the ninth century and one of the eleventh (F. F. Bruce, *The New Testament Documents: Are they Reliable?* [Inter-Varsity Press:London 1943]).

In stark contrast we now possess over *twenty-four thousand* whole or partial surviving manuscripts of the New Testament alone.

The dramatic discovery of the Dead Sea Scrolls by a Bedouin shepherd boy in the caves at Qumran, shortly after the Second World War, has been extremely important. These Hebrew texts of the Old Testament have vividly confirmed the accuracy with which the Old Testament had been transcribed through the centuries.

It is interesting to note that many modern historians possess a high opinion of the historians of the Roman world. The writers of the Gospels came from this same tradition.

Two Scandinavian scholars, Harald Riesenfeld and Birger Gerhardsson, have drawn a close analogy between the teaching style of Jesus and that of the Jewish rabbis. The rabbis ensured that their sayings *The accuracy of Jewish oral tradition* were passed on accurately by word of mouth among their followers.

Gerhardsson suggests that Jesus adopted the same method to ensure that his disciples learned his teaching by heart, and would accurately transmit it to their own followers.

In the Jewish religion it was customary for the student to memorise the rabbi's teaching. A good pupil was like 'a plastered cistern that loses not a drop' (*Mishne*, Aboth, II 8). Many, therefore, argued that there was not enough time for the words of Christ to be lost between the original teaching and its recording by the gospel writers.

The popular argument that because the Bible was produced nearly two thousand years ago it must necessarily be full of errors and discrepancies, has largely been discredited.

When the trustworthiness of the Scriptures is tested by the same methods as are employed for other historical documents, then their reliability outweighs that of all other contemporary histories.

In fact, our developing knowledge of life in first-century Palestine indicates that the Gospels represent more reliable accounts than had first been supposed. A large number of important geographical and social details have substantially confirmed the truth of the biblical records.

The Bible has been subjected to closer critical study than any other book in human history. Form analysis, textual examination, archaeological discoveries, source criticism, linguistic analysis and tests for historical accuracy have all been employed in attempts to examine the truth or otherwise of the biblical material. At a cruder level it has been banned, parodied and burned, and yet the claim that the Bible is God speaking to us, is alive and well. Today it is more widely read than at any time in history. Translated into over two thousand languages it not only survives – it flourishes!

As Michael Green has succinctly commented, 'The Bible writers themselves believed they were inspired by God, Jesus believed they were, the church believed they were. Some modern scholars do not believe this. The issue is plain; the choice is ours'. (ed. M. Green, *The Truth of God Incarnate* [Hodder and Stoughton: London, 1978]).

It has often been noted that throughout the centuries the most serious damage has always been inflicted on the church from the inside, rather than from the outside. Today, attacked by objections from society, and undermined from within, the greatest miracle is that Christianity has managed to survive.

Yet it has! Two thousand years of objection have failed to overthrow the Christian faith or the truth of its message. Its critics are not ignored, but answered – and despite the objectors, the number of Christians keeps growing; each day nearly ninety more people are added to the church. Once the church would have silenced the objectors, today the gospel spreads through the answers to the challenges. For truth will ultimately never be silenced.

4
Fact and Faith

Truth is more than objective reality. Truth is to be lived. In this chapter we examine the ways in which the Holy Spirit has inspired the Bible, and the ways in which he works in our lives.

Fact and Faith

We arrive at the truth, not by the reason only,
but also by the heart.

Pascal

At the heart of the Christian faith lies the word of God which he interprets to us today. This is truth which lives in experience; a faith which is based on facts.

Christian truth must never be segregated into a purely emotional or solely intellectual response. It cannot be dismissed as spiritual passion or merely the message contained in the pages of a book. Our convictions are to be lived as well as learned, both experienced and understood.

Central to the gospel is the unique combination of the Spirit and the word. These two separate principles are united; rather than contradict one another they must exist in partnership together. Neither is the truth by themselves; that truth specifically is discovered in Jesus. Both the Spirit and the word bear testimony to the truth that is only found in him.

A depth of meaning is hidden in the simple rhyme:

> If you have the word and not the Spirit you'll dry up,
> If you have the Spirit and not the word you'll blow up.
> If you have the word and the Spirit together you'll grow up.

Adherence to the word alone gives a slavish submission to text, while commitment to the voice of our spirit deprives us of the checks and balances provided by Scripture. It has been relatively easy for one section of the church to imply that, 'God wants your heart, not your head'. Meanwhile others affirm, 'The heart is unreliable, only scripture provides us with a safe foundation'. In fact both are required.

Some years ago a close personal friend, Mike Morris, and I were both working in Youth for Christ. We appointed an experienced and professional secretary, Brenda Day, to assist us. However, in an embryonic work the absence of a suitable typewriter for her passed unnoticed.

Mike had only recently been appointed as my assistant and was keen to see the work progress. As a relatively young Christian, fresh out of Oxford University, Mike believed what he read in Scripture about God who provides for our needs. So he ordered a sophisticated typewriter from a firm of office suppliers at a cost of around six hundred pounds. The only problem was that we had no money in the bank to meet this obligation!

As Mike prayed over the issue he sensed a genuine confirmation in his spirit that the word which spoke of God's provision would be proved correct. The typewriter duly arrived, and so did the bill. There remained no money to pay for it. So Mike kept on praying.

A few days later we were driving together up the M1. Stopping at Rothersthorpe Service Station, Mike left the car to pay for petrol. As we continued up the road Mike casually commented, 'Guess what I found? A wad of ten pound notes on the floor by the petrol pump.' When I asked as to how much was involved, we counted sixty ten pound notes.

The matter was duly reported to the police who suggested that as we worked for a charity we should hold onto the money till a claimant emerged. None ever did, and eventually we were assured that the money was ours – and Brenda had her typewriter. This may explain the enquiring gaze of many full-time Christian workers at the floor of the forecourt of Rothersthorpe Service Area! It also illustrates that where word and Spirit combine, the humanly impossible does happen!

God's truth is neither abstract or remote. It is witnessed in the here and now. Christian testimony throughout the ages is that as people have implemented the truths of Scripture in their daily lives, they have been found to be right. The commands of Scripture work for our good, the promises of Scripture are fulfilled. By the activity of the Holy Spirit, God comes to us in order that truth might emerge from theory and become living reality. What God has declared in Scripture, he will fulfil among his people.

The truth within

The Bible insists that God is a God of truth. He cannot lie (Heb 6:18); he is faithful and trustworthy (Deut 32:4; 2 Sam 7:28; Ps 146:6); and will always be true and right in his actions and judgements (Rom 3:4).

When Jesus was preparing the disciples for his impending death and departure, he promised not to leave them alone. Rather than leave them as orphans he would send his Holy Spirit (Jn 14:8). This Holy Spirit is never less than God himself. He is the Spirit of Jesus, Spirit of the Lord, and the gift of the Father (Acts 16:7; Phil 1:19; 1 Kings 18:12; Lk 11:13). When Peter confronts Ananias he declares, 'you have lied to the Holy Spirit… you have not lied to men but to God' (Acts 5:3-4).

The Holy Spirit possesses all the attributes of God. He is omniscient – all-knowing; omnipotent – all-powerful; *The nature of* and omnipresent – everywhere simultaneously (1 Cor *the Holy* 2:10-11; Lk 1:35-37; Ps 139:7). Everywhere in *Spirit* Scripture it is assumed that the Holy Spirit is God.

God is Trinity; therefore a God of truth, whose Son is the truth, must possess a Spirit whose nature and character is truth as well. That is why the Holy Spirit is termed the Spirit of truth (Jn 14:17; 15:26; 16:13; 1 Jn 4:6).

This Spirit of truth is Christ's gift to believers (Acts 2:32-33). The Holy Spirit is a person, not a thing, yet we refer to him loosely as 'he', for the noun used in Scripture is feminine in Hebrew, and neuter in Greek. He, as God, transcends human categories of gender. The Spirit comes alongside us in order to lead us into all truth. In fact he is there to teach us all that we need to know (Jn 14:26; 16:13).

The Holy Spirit's work in us   The Holy Spirit communicates directly with us bringing revelation, authentication and inspiration of truth (Jn 16:13; 1 Sam 10:10). Far from working by remote control, he brings us into God's family, so that we are spiritual orphans no longer (Jn 14:18; Rom 8:11, 15-17). All who have committed their lives to Jesus Christ will therefore know the Holy Spirit at work within their lives, making his home in them.

In this way God brings his truth to live within us. By this means the Spirit of truth is in our lives to teach us God's requirements, to bring glory and honour to Jesus (Jn 16:8-10, 14).

Most of us are only too aware of the vast difference between knowing what we should do in life, and actually achieving it. We often understand truth, but struggle to match up to its requirements.

Paul bemoaned his inability to do what is good, but rejoiced that the Holy Spirit within him could achieve what he could never manage alone (Rom 7:14 – 8:4). Living according to the principles of the sinful nature results in death, but to live by the Spirit guarantees life, 'Because those who are led by the Spirit of God are sons of God' (Rom 8:13-14).

The Holy Spirit goes beyond teaching us about the truth. He alone gives us the strength to live in the way that God intends. He leads us and guides us (Acts 13:2; 15:28). The Spirit of truth equips us for service (Judg 14:6; 2 Kings 2:9; Acts 1:8); he supplies us as individuals with the power of God (Ex 35:31; Mic 3:8; Acts 4:8; 9:17; Eph 5:18).

In providing us with all that we need to live by the truth, the Holy Spirit offers us spiritual resources (1 Cor 12:8-10; Gal 5:22-23). We all have to recognise and value both the gifts and fruit which the Holy Spirit provides for us, and then works out within our lives.

We will never properly understand the significance of either the gifts or fruit until we see the truth which Scripture reveals about the Holy Spirit. It is who he is that determines what he does. Not content with leading us into truth he provides us with the practical necessities required to live by the truth.

The Spirit and the word

Scripture is given to us in order that we may know what God wants from us. The Spirit enables us to begin to live that way. Christians should never be guilty of preferring God's explanation of his will in Scripture, to his revelation of himself by his Spirit. We were never given a Trinity of Father, Son and Holy Scripture.

In avoiding this error, many have swung too far in the opposite direction. If we judge the value of what we do in terms of the satisfaction it gives us, then we will have been guilty of sacrificing truth on the altar of experience. *Truth and experience*

The Spirit is given to lead us to the truth. We must never replace truth by experience, or be content with truth instead of experience. The two should always be held in harmony together.

During the seventeenth century a Puritan author, William Gurnall, summed it up neatly in these words, 'Some by truth mean truth of doctrine; others will have it truth of heart, sincerity; they, I think, are best that compromise both ... one will not do without the other.'

To overemphasise truth will lead us into a dead formalism. We know theory from the past, but lack the vitality of actively knowing God in present-day reality.

> In this hour of all-but-universal darkness one cheering gleam appears: within the fold of conservative Christianity there are to be found increasing numbers of persons whose religious lives are marked by a growing hunger after God Himself. They are eager for spiritual realities and will not be put off with words, nor will they be content with correct 'interpretations' of truth. *A hunger for God*
>
> They are athirst for God, and they will not be satisfied till they have drunk deep at the Fountain of Living Water. This is the only real harbinger of revival which I have been able to detect anywhere on the religious horizon. (A. W. Tozer, *The Pursuit of God* [STL: Bromley, 1987]).

To major on experience without mooring it to a secure foundation leaves us open to any extreme idea which comes along. We are often more gullible than we think – and can follow personalities in what they say, rather than measure their content at the bar of Scripture. For we are always to test all things in order to ascertain whether they are truly of God – or not! (1 Jn 4:1).

The cult massacres of recent years – in Jonestown, Guyana, in Switzerland and in Canada – act as a stark reminder that God has given us an invaluable measure of truth – the Bible. We neglect its authority over all our ideas, doctrines and practices at our peril, for we would then permit other authorities to stake their claim to our allegiance.

The Spirit also teaches us the way to handle truth. For it is the *How to handle truth* Holy Spirit who provides the grace and wisdom to avoid bigotry and arrogance, yet still be able to contend for the truth it presents.

> Twin dangers confront the Christian concerned with defining and promulgating biblical truth. The first is pugnaciousness. The line between contending for the faith and being contentious about the faith is extremely thin... The second danger is less easy to recognise, but is no less insidious. It is a kind of arrogant apathy that bolsters a mindset less interested in the truth than its pursuits. It involves a fine balancing of all opinions in such a way that a person is somehow impolite to insist that one opinion has the ring of truth, and, conversely, the others are to that degree false... (D. A. Carson & J. D. Woodbridge, eds., *Scripture and Truth* [IVP: Leicester, 1983]).

To follow the dictates of experience, or to be content with bare truth at the expense of living reality, are equal errors. It is the Holy Spirit who provides the resources we need to hold the two in glorious tension together.

More than 'The Good Book'

Christians have traditionally maintained that the Bible is no mere literary exercise. It is devalued when referred to as just *The authority of Scripture* a 'good book'. For the historic belief of the church is that the Bible is the word of God written.

It is held that Scripture is 'without error in all that it affirms'

(Lausanne Covenant). Its teaching is infallibly true, vital to the well-being of the church and capable of reasonable defence at all times and against all attacks.

The Bible, Christians believe, is accurate and reliable. The Holy Spirit himself inspired what was written and we similarly need his direction as we read its pages today.

This belief stems from its birthplace, for the Christian conviction is that the Bible originated in the heart of God. We can therefore have confidence in 'The divine inspiration of the Holy Scripture and its consequent entire trustworthiness and supreme authority in all matters of faith and conduct' (Evangelical Alliance: Basis of Faith).

There are three reasons why the Bible brings us the truth about God.

(a) *It is inspired by God Himself.* The claim of the Bible is that it does not originate with those who wrote it. It is not just a library of books produced by human authorship, but the compilation of the Spirit of God. The Spirit breathed the word, and therefore that word is truth.

Often Scripture does not appear to be written by one divine author. The different literary styles, educations, personalities, professions and cultural backgrounds of the human authors are all allowed to shine through. *Many authors but one Author* God's purpose in Scripture is communication, and the consistency in variety provided by history, poetry, prophecy and doctrine indicates the master hand of the guiding Holy Spirit using the gifts of very different people.

Divine inspiration means that God has breathed his word through writers who acted as his spokespersons. They felt that, while writing, they were giving expression to the truth of God. Far from feeling alone, they considered themselves to have been inspired by God in their writing. These were no ordinary authors, for they were clearly conscious that the Holy Spirit was moving upon them to enable each one to express God's truth in their own words (Ex 4:10-15; Deut 4:2; Jer 1:7-9; 1 Cor 2:13; 14:37; 1 Pet 1:10,11; 2 Pet 1:20-21).

The New Testament writers claimed the same inspiration for themselves as for the authors of the books of the Old Testament (Acts 1:16; 28:25; 2 Tim 3:16-17).

This does not mean that God used people as human dictating machines, obliterating their own personalities. Their literary style, vocabulary and culture remained their own – yet their testimony was that of those who 'spoke from God as they were carried along by the Holy Spirit' (2 Pet 1:21).

(b) *It offers revelation.* Scripture does not merely transmit information about ourselves. It provides insights into the nature and character of God, while telling us about life in the way the Creator intended that it should be lived.

God's initiative to us The word 'revelation' comes from a Latin word which means 'removing a veil'. It indicates that God himself has taken the initiative to make his nature and character known to us. At the moment of Jesus' death the Temple curtain was torn in two, from the top to the bottom, unveiling the Holy of Holies (Mt 27:51). This was essential, for God was not now to be preserved in a building, but his life would be lived within his people.

We cannot find God for ourselves, so God reveals himself to us. This he has done in his creation, by his Son, and through the words of Scripture. The Bible can, therefore, be legitimately regarded as the Christian's handbook. It is ever-relevant, the source of direction into truth.

As such it acts as spiritual food (Deut 8:3; Ps 19:10; 1 Pet 2:2; Heb 5:13-14 AV). It is our sword of the Spirit, and a hammer against our enemies (Jer 23:29; Eph 6:17; Heb 4:12). The Bible is life-changing, it redirects us intellectually, morally, spiritually and practically. As Paul instructed his young disciple Timothy, 'All Scripture is God-breathed and is useful for teaching, rebuking, correcting and training in righteousness' (2 Tim 3:16).

The whole movement of the Bible is to make us mature men and women for God. It reveals God's intention to teach us how to live for him and for each other (Rom 15:4), and therefore makes us 'wise unto salvation' (Ps 19:7-11; 2 Tim 3:14-15).

This revelation of God gives teaching, grace and support in order that we may be able to do God's will (2 Tim 3:16-17). It provides the means to test spiritual experience and gifting (Acts 17:11; 1 Thess 5:21), while equipping us to resist Satan and his temptations (Mt 4:4-10). Instead of leaving us to our own devices, the Bible introduces us to the heart and intentions of God.

(c) *It possesses unique authority.* If Scripture contains, as it claims, a divine revelation given by divine inspiration, then it possesses authority over us. This is true whether we recognise it or not!

God's word has to carry God's authority. As God he does not possess the ability to lie, for that would be to deny his own consistent character. Because of who he is, we have to believe what he says (Num 23:19; 1 Sam 15:29; Tit 1:2; Heb 6:18).

The Bible's own claims for its authority

The degree of authority which the authors gave to the Scripture they wrote is astounding. The prophets gave testimony to the revelation they received, so they confidently claimed to utter and write words given by God alone (Ex 19:3; 20:21; 24:18; 33:11; Isa 6:8; Jer 1:5-9; Ezek 2:7; Hos 4:1; Amos 2:1). The apostles saw themselves as divinely directed, with their words proceeding from God (Heb 10:15-17).

The New Testament Scriptures were viewed as Christ-given, and the writers as Spirit-led (Gal 1:11-12; Jn 14:16-26; 16:12-15; 1 Cor 2:13). The apostles regarded their own teaching, writing and commands as divinely authoritative and binding upon the churches (1 Cor 2:9-13; 14:37; Gal 1:6-10; Eph 2:20), to be read aloud in the churches (Col 4:16), and pondered just as 'the other scriptures' of the Old Testament (2 Pet 3:16).

Clearly this combination of inspiration, revelation and authority places the Scriptures in a class of their own. They announced truth and claimed to be truth. It is difficult to accept the content of their teaching without recognising *the claims that the Bible contains for its own authenticity.*

There are those who would wish to disagree. Attempts have been made to erode confidence in the truth and accuracy of the biblical records when taken at their face value. For example, many scholars have come to regard the Old Testament books as a collection of myth, legend, saga and fable, drawn from various written sources and oral folk-tales.

Schleiermacher maintained that feeling rather than fact lay at the heart of faith. He saw religion as a 'feeling of absolute dependence' upon God. His position of 'subjective individualism' saw the Bible as useful, but not essential, to the Christian faith. It was spirit rather than word that was important, for personal faith could not be based on Scripture, but was located in our own experience of God.

Many of the so-called 'contradictions' in the biblical records can be explained in ways other than liberal scholars have suggested. These interpretations are usually far more straightforward than the more fanciful alternatives which have been proposed.

Difficulties in the biblical text

In John's gospel the story of the cleansing of the Temple takes place at the beginning of the ministry of Jesus (Jn 2:13-16). In Luke it takes place at the end (Lk 19:45-46). It is suggested that Luke's record is chronologically accurate. John simply reconstructed the order of the material in order to make a theological point.

John may indeed not have adhered to a strict chronology. His record would not be any the less true. As Dr John Drane has commented, 'There is, however, no logical reason at all why a story or piece of teaching that conveys a practical or theological message has to be historically false' (J. Drane, *Introducing the New Testament* [Lion: Tring, 1986]).

Other difficulties receive an easier response. In Acts 17:6 Luke refers to the civil authorities of Thessalonica as 'politarchs'. Until recently this term had not been discovered in classical literature. Luke was therefore held to be wrong. However, nineteen inscriptions have now been found which make use of this title. Five of them are in reference to Thessalonica!

The plain fact is that the writers of Scripture would scarcely have fabricated their accounts. The Jewish understanding of history might differ from ours, but they would never have wished to obscure or discredit their message. They would never have wanted the Bible to be regarded as 'The Good Book', rather as God's revelation of himself for the whole of humankind.

Help from heaven

The Spirit and the word

If God had left us alone with a textbook, that would not have been enough. To know the will of God is a million miles removed from having the power and the ability to obey it. For God has not revealed his purposes in order that we might merely understand them; he requires our cooperation in their fulfilment. This we could never achieve unaided!

It would be impossible to obey Scripture and live according to its instructions without the Holy Spirit. While he inspired the original authors, he gives to God's people the energy and power required to live according to the truth.

These are the twin aspects of the Christian life. We live according to God's word through the energy of the Holy Spirit. We do not have to survive alone; we have help from God himself.

It is the Holy Spirit who is the author of revelation, who brought God's message to the prophets (Is 61:1-4; Acts 2). He was in charge of its inspiration (1 Cor 2:9-10). Through the internal activity of the Spirit in the life of the believer, he gives us the power to appropriate God's truth for ourselves (Rom 8:14-17; 1 Cor 2:1-16; 1 Thess 1:5, 2:13; 1 Jn 2:27; 5:9).

It is impossible to underestimate the significance of the work of the Holy Spirit in bringing truth *into* the life of the believer. He it is who takes truth which has objective *The task of the Spirit* existence apart from us, and brings it to live inside us. He applies the teaching of Scripture to our daily lives and reflects the Father's response to our prayers for help and direction from God.

Before conversion, as in the biblical cases of Zacchaeus, Cornelius, and the Ethiopian eunuch, the Holy Spirit is preparing the ground for the conversion of the individual. It is the Holy Spirit who brings conviction of sin, righteousness and judgement (Jn 16:8).

At conversion the Holy Spirit comes to live in every believer (Rom 8:9). He is the giver of new life (Rom 8:11; Jn 3:5; Tit 3:5), and the seal of our salvation (2 Cor 1:22).

After conversion the Holy Spirit takes the 'new material' of the new convert and begins to mould our lives into the image of Jesus (2 Cor 3:18).

When the New Testament speaks of 'an indwelling Holy Spirit' in the life of the believer, it is introducing a concept unknown in other major world religions. Most faiths look to 'holy men' exceptionally in touch with God or gods. Christianity excludes this special category. Through the Holy Spirit all believers may know the truth, because he is internalised in our lives. This means that we do not have to be afraid of the Holy

Spirit. Far from it. Instead we need to cultivate his presence, surrender our lives to his control, and receive all that he wants to give and do within us.

The Holy Spirit revealed in the Bible is the same Holy Spirit whom we encounter today. So we can expect him to be active in our lives to achieve those same objectives which were present when he moved within the early church. For this we need to pray, and be prepared to willingly respond in lives of daily discipleship.

The truth that we encounter in the Bible is to be lived through the power of the Holy Spirit. That is the gift and intention of God.

We are called to be God's people. This means that we are under obligation to obey his directions (Lk 11:28; Acts 5:29; Heb 5:9). These are revealed through Scripture (Ps 19:7-14), and can only be lived by the energising of his Holy Spirit. The will and power of God are inseparable for the believer, they enable us to live by facts and faith!

5

Truth to Live By

If truth is not universal, but individual, then where are the limits to individual freedom? In this chapter we consider the implications of the 'death of truth' for public and private morality. If individualism rules, is there any possibility for a widespread ethical consensus? Can Christians reasonably expect secular society to adopt God's laws?

Truth to Live By

Truth forever on the scaffold, Wrong forever on the throne,
Yet that scaffold sways the future and behind the dim unknown,
Standeth God within the shadow, keeping watch above
*   his own.*

James Russell Lowell.

Karen was seventeen, and she was pregnant. The shock was immense, she had never faced a situation of this magnitude before, and had no idea what to do about it. Her two closest girlfriends were very concerned. 'Rotten luck, and from only a one-night stand' was their sympathetic comment. She had to tell the guy, and he promised to stand by her, but then didn't seem to be around anymore.

Faced with a critical choice she had no guidelines from which to operate. So there she was, three months away from going to college, and six months short of becoming a mother.

Her parents accepted the news of the loss of her virginity with equanimity. It was her life, she could choose the way she wanted to live. After all, most of their friends had children who were adopting exactly the same lifestyle. Why bother to tell them anyway?

It was the second part of her story that created consternation.

They learned of her pregnancy with visible horror. Karen's mother urged her to visit their local GP. He would know what could be done to resolve the issue.

So Karen found herself sitting in the doctor's surgery pouring out her story. She was not given much advice. Her situation was accepted as being normal and quite straightforward.

Karen was told that the big danger lay in the damage that would be done to her career. Her future could be ruined, but there was a simple solution. Abortion was a straightforward operation which should not have a prejudicial effect on her subsequent fertility. Counselling was available to assist her through this period. The GP suggested that the main difficulty lay in hospital waiting lists. She was eleven weeks pregnant and the operation had to take place within the next thirteen weeks. This could not be guaranteed within the NHS system, but there was an excellent local private clinic. The costs involved would amount to two hundred pounds.

The Family Planning Clinic were equally explicit with their advice. Karen's body was her own, and she could choose what should happen. This was a time to think of herself. No judgement was passed on what she had done: it was the future that mattered.

Still Karen felt unsettled and uncertain. She pleaded with her parents for more time to think it over. In her heart she wasn't sure that abortion was necessarily a good idea. So Karen decided to get a second opinion. Occasionally she went to church and liked the vicar, so she thought that he might be able to help her.

Sitting there in his study Karen explained her situation. The vicar's advice was simple and to the point. Within her womb was an embryonic child. She had no right to take that life away. Sex outside of marriage was never God's intention, but we are human and do make mistakes. In his love God would freely forgive her, but she should have the baby and then seek for it to be adopted.

The vicar was a sincere evangelical, and being a supporter of CARE, he knew something of the issues involved. He suggested that Karen should visit the local social services to gain details of how an adoption could be arranged. He assured her that after having the baby she could surrender the child immediately if she wished. He also warned that the operation could lead to the emotional trauma of post-abortion syndrome. The vicar prayed for Karen, and she began to sense the warmth of God's love and forgiveness.

The situation at home was rather different. Karen's mum was anxious to know what was happening. Her advice for her daughter was quite explicit. She was going to college, and although this could be postponed for a year, it could hamper her future career. Adoption represented one possibility, but motherhood produced its own tensions. Abortion would be simpler, it removed personal stigma or embarrassment, and could be arranged – the family would pay the bill. Karen must consider her own rights and needs. The interests of the foetus within her were barely considered.

Karen chose the abortion. Her GP, along with another doctor at the practice, sanctioned the operation on the grounds that 'there was risk of injury to the physical or mental health of the woman.'

The idea that this choice might be right or wrong did not emerge. For on this kind of issue two world views collide with each other. The Christian view of morality urges that there are absolute standards of truth which apply to every generation; contemporary society insists that every individual has the right to independent choice of action for themselves.

Do your own thing!

This glib phrase from the sixties summarises the modern attitude. Each of us possesses the right to choose truth for ourselves. There are no absolutes that apply to everyone, for every person has the right to determine their own course of action. Heterosexual or homosexual lifestyle, fidelity or promiscuity, equity or exploitation – in each case, we are told, the choice lies with yourself.

Unfortunately this argument is fatally flawed. For society might want to resist the temptation to impose limits on the individual, but still finds it necessary to do so. The rule of law, protection of the disadvantaged and oppressed, and limitations on exploitation all illustrate the point. *The limits to individual freedom*

Instead of removing the obstacles to independent action, society has simply altered the boundaries. So human sexuality is given free expression, but paedophilia is outlawed. A man imprisoned for theft from his neighbour will see little inconsistency in beating up a man jailed for child abuse. Rather than the removal of all restrictions, we have simply chosen to remodel them to suit our own convenience.

Contemporary ideas of truth to live by, the ethical understanding by which we conduct our lives, have become a matter of personal choice. Right and wrong is reduced to the viewpoint or preference of the individual concerned.

All of us are affected by the culture and presuppositions of the society in which we live. Today's regular diet of soap operas, media comment and workplace conversation have become vehicles for the perspectives of secular philosophy. Such ideas, which once were unusual, have now emerged from the seclusion of academia into the mainstream of everyday life. The danger is that we absorb the presuppositions behind *East Enders, Home and Away* or *News at Ten* without recognising their origins, and without submitting them to biblical evaluation and assessment.

Morality – ancient and modern

In fact there is little modern about current freethinking ideas. The book of Judges spoke of a time when 'every man did that which was right in his own eyes' (Judg 21:25 AV) – and that was around 1100 BC!

The ancient Greek philosopher, Protagoras, claimed that 'man is the measure of all things'. By this statement he meant that the will of each person establishes the standard for them of what is right or wrong. Therefore the morally right thing to do is that which is morally right for me. I must never try to inflict my standards on others, for what is right for me may be wrong for someone else. It is interesting to note the contemporary ring in such statements; modern in tone, they predate the birth of Jesus Christ!

Another Greek philosopher, Thrasymachus, is credited with the view that, 'justice is the interest of the stronger party'. This defines what is morally right in terms of who has the power. As George Bernard Shaw cynically commented in his play *St Joan*, 'God is on the side of the big battalions'. Twentieth-century tyrants like Stalin, Hitler and Pol Pot vividly demonstrate that this view is not dead.

Aristotle defined morality in terms of moderation. The right thing is always found in the moderate course of action. He saw temperance as the mean between indulgence and insensibility. Similarly courage was the halfway house between fear and aggression.

While there is some truth in this last view, and the Bible endorses moderation as a virtue (Phil 4:5), there are always times when extreme action is right. Generosity, gratitude and love are not intended to be dispensed in moderate amounts! Yet today's society follows Aristotle in approving tolerance of all things in moderation, without distinguishing between that which is good and bad. As one ethicist has commented, 'Moderation is at best only a general guide for action, not a universal ethical law' (N. Geisler, *Christian Ethics* [Apollos: Leicester, 1989]).

The fourth-century BC Epicurean philosophers asserted that everything which brings pleasure must be morally right, and that which creates pain is morally wrong. This hedonistic (pleasure-seeking) lifestyle wins modern approval best summarised in the T-shirt message, 'If it feels good, do it'. The emphasis is on the immediate; the long-term consequences are less carefully considered.

Even before the earliest law codes were written down, human society had developed its own understanding of how people should behave towards each other. These views of right and wrong were always influenced by the religious beliefs of that society. For example, those who believe in reincarnation could never consent to kill any animal. Or, if a god is displeased with society and withholds the rainfall, then human sacrifices to appease his wrath could be a good thing.

Western society has been dominated, for most of the last two thousand years, by Christianity. Our Christian heritage created a belief in fixed standards *Christian ideas of morality* of right and wrong which were established by a Creator God. These were regarded as superior to those which existed in all other faiths and cultures.

While people often disobeyed God's laws, the impact of almost universal church attendance created a Christianised society. At times faith might not have been very personal or deep, but the general . population knew what God demanded from them. These standards became regarded as 'normal' behaviour.

The 18th century revolution   The influence of the church lay at the heart of the system. During the eighteenth century an internal revolution took place. People began to reject traditional teaching and started to think for themselves.

Two major strands of influence emerged. The academic world was divided between 'empiricists' who believed all helpful knowledge came from experience, and 'rationalists' who believed reason was the source of all knowledge; while followers of the Enlightenment – who stressed tolerance, commonsense and reasonableness – saw human reason as the ultimate standard for determining truth and morals. To them, something could only be true if it could be demonstrated that it was reasonable, whether God said it or not.

The results were enormous, not only on society then, but also for today. For while much current thinking echoes ancient opinion, these more modern influences have been enormously significant. The traditional ethics of Western society, which had been based on the Bible, were now open to challenge. Humankind was to be its own arbiter of right and wrong. I could now determine truth for myself.

The death of the truth

The sense of self-confidence in human reason was shattered by the horrors of trench warfare during the First World War. This was followed by economic depression, unemployment, the rise of Fascism and Communism, and then the ultimate denial of human reason – the nuclear bomb.

Once it had been easy to regard the human race as the only self-conscious, self-determined being in the universe – the rulers of all! Now the question came, 'If humankind is self-determining, why do we act as we do, and how can we create such appalling violence and devastation?'

It was a short step to conclude that it could not be our fault. Our actions are obviously influenced by our genetic make-up and the effects of our environment. Therefore we are purely *The abdication* the result of external forces and the past, over which *of responsibility* we have no control. So even the concept of human freedom is an illusion. We cannot recognise why we take certain decisions, but suffer from the 'domino-effect' of all that is happening around us. The good news was that no-one could be held responsible for their own actions. The bad news was that life became causeless and purposeless, Godless, meaningless and absurd.

Into this apparent world of universal darkness came *The rise of* a ray of hope. Post-war Western Europe embraced an *existentialism* existential and relativistic perspective which affirmed that the world might be absurd, but as an individual human being I could possess meaning and personal significance. It was reasoned that 'I cannot tell you what truth is, for you must decide this for yourself, but when you do, you must decide for yourself and all people'. This did not mean imposing one's personal choices on everyone, but committing yourself to a course of action which you believed to be right for you, and for everyone. This individualistic concept has been extended to produce a popular view which totally emphasises our own subjective world. A lonely existence in a private world where our individual choices and decisions make us into the people we are today. There is no truth outside of ourselves – we are the truth for us, otherwise truth is dead.

Each of us is understood as being a blank piece of paper. On this has been written our experiences of life, which have combined to constitute our knowledge of the truth. So truth is entirely dependent on our own personal experience. There is no ultimate truth, only what we discover works in our own lives.

So one individual may choose to engage in a promiscuous heterosexual lifestyle. Another can develop a homosexual relationship. Others may choose to marry and remain faithful to one partner. Each way, the relativist argues, is appropriate to the person who chooses to adopt it – and each is equally valid.

Such a theory inevitably results in the destruction of truth as Christians have known it. No room remains for the existence of any absolute, objective standard of morality which can apply to each person in whatever situation they find themselves. It denies the authority of the imperatives outlined in the Bible. The individual simply becomes his, or her, own ethic.

Truth is therefore regarded as only applying to the individual concerned. There is no concept of 'true truth', just truth for me – and my truth can never be yours, or vice versa, unless it is embraced by your own experience. Each individual is to be left alone with their own decisions or dilemmas.

Can we find any ethical consensus?
In his famous lecture on existentialism, Jean-Paul Sartre, the last existentialist to avow the title, tells of his refusal to advise a young man facing an ethical dilemma. In the subsequent discussion with the philosophers who heard the lecture, two criticised him. 'You should have told him what to do,' they said. One of these was a Christian, the other a Communist. 'Existentialists make a virtue of not knowing what to do' (Carl Michalson, 'Existentialist Ethics' in J. Macquarrie & J. Childress ed. *A New Dictionary of Christian Ethics* [SCM: London, 1986]).

In the absence of clear-cut guidelines, each has to live from their own perception. In his 1990 Reith lecture the Chief Rabbi, Jonathan Sachs, summed up the dilemma of our modern world. 'Does morality in any significant sense exist any more? We speak of right and wrong, good and bad, justice and rights. But these are all words which were once thought to refer to objective principles, and it is these that we believe do not exist' (a point of view which he strenuously rejected).

Situational ethics
In the absence of agreed principles or standards society has resorted to a policy of situational ethics. If no conduct is good or bad in itself, then each person must determine what is right or wrong in every individual situation – a process which can be compared to navigating in the dark without a chart or a compass! Truth becomes a matter of sincerity rather than clarity. If someone is sincerely convinced that a course of action is right for them, then they are beyond contradiction.

Faced with life devoid of basic absolutes, society has adopted a variety of alternative concepts of truth.

* The hedonist devotes his life to the pursuit of personal pleasure.

* The materialist bases expectations on a free-market economy.

* The utilitarian looks to the greatest happiness principle through the creation of laws designed to provide the greatest happiness for the greatest number.

* The individualist is determined to do it 'my way'. For most people this consists of rejecting any one code, and simply adopting whatever appears to be the most suitable to them in a specific situation.

These options can be applauded as a means of resisting collective dictatorship and protecting the rights of the individual, but is this a sufficiently valid argument?

We have generated a society in which truth is relegated to the level of a minority concern, only receiving headline exposure when a public figure is exposed for dishonesty. Words like integrity and upright character have become highly unfashionable. As for honesty – try witnessing the reaction on returning a mistaken surplus of change!

Any idea of protecting people from themselves leads to accusations of censorship or 'nannying', and the powerless are left to fend for themselves. A moral code which sanctions an individualistic basis for all behaviour, leaves little room to acknowledge responsibility for the elderly, deprived, abused or homeless.

If truth is bound up in the individual, then ideas of self-actualisation and self-esteem achieve paramount importance. Ideas of 'home' and 'family' become reduced to a location, rather than participation in a community. Selfishness can easily become a way of life – and God is firmly dismissed from the scene.

In pursuit of the truth

Trying to grasp hold of truth in a secular world is like attempting to seize a bar of wet soap. Just when you think you have hold of it, the soap slips out of your grasp. Secular views of truth are based on human reason and experience, coupled with individual hopes and desires – and therefore are constantly changing.

The Christian understanding of truth is radically different. It is firmly rooted in the character of God and his revelation of his will and purpose in Scripture. Biblical standards of truth and conduct are God-centred. They stand in stark contrast to Greek and Latin roots of the word 'ethics' which simply mean 'custom'. So instead of conforming to individual habit or majority opinion, Scripture insists that the Christian must live by God's truth and its requirements, rather than personal desires.

The reason for this is that God's truth is absolute and unchangeable, because that is the nature of his moral character. God remains the same (Mal 3:6; Jas 1:17), so those codes of practice which he declared, like the Ten Commandments, remain as valid for today as for when they were first given.

God's universal laws

These moral requirements apply to all humankind, because each person has been created in the image of God (Gen 1:27; Col 3:10; Jas 3:9). For this reason commandments like 'do not commit adultery' are not subject to any given situation, but are absolute for every time, every place and every one. They will not vary, because to contravene this kind of instruction from our Creator is to deny the very will and character of God.

One word of warning is necessary. Scripture also contains specific instructions which relate to a particular time and place, and must therefore be viewed differently. The dietary laws of the Old Testament did not usually relate to God's moral character, but to the health needs of the people in a given situation. This is an important distinction because otherwise we may find ourselves having to adopt the cleansing rituals of Leviticus! These specific laws may have little immediate relevance to us, but the Spirit behind them still has much to teach us. He alone will help us to determine what applies to today, and give us the courage and strength to follow his direction.

Moral law and the created order

The Christian message boldly declares that God has revealed both himself and his will and purpose for his created order. In fact, even those who are unaware of the gospel, still have the revelation of God contained in conscience, nature and creation (Ps 19:1-6; Rom 1:19-20). Failure to see that God is the one to whom we must answer does not excuse anyone (Rom 2:14-15).

As Norman Geisler has acutely observed, 'Even if unbelievers do not have the moral law in their minds, they still have it written on their hearts. Even if they do not know it by way of cognition, they show it by way of inclination' (N. Geisler *op cit*).

It is because we live in the world made by God that each of us is under obligation to live in it the way that he intended. Failure to do so will produce its own bitter, but inevitable consequences.

Making this kind of observation leaves evangelical Christians open to the charge of being lacklustre killjoys, or worse. How dare we seek to impose our religion on everyone else? Yet the simple Christian statement is that the whole creation is the Lord's. We worship the Creator whose concerns transcend the Christian community alone.

Many would be shocked to read the bold statement, *An example* 'AIDS is the judgement of God'. For the contemporary *of AIDS* journalist this neat phrase offered a striking indictment of the loveless, condemning attitude that they felt would be the reaction of today's Christians to the horrors of the AIDS epidemic.

These few words conjured up the picture of a harsh, arbitrary and vindictive God pouring out his wrath on innocent victims. This surely was the posture that many Christians would adopt towards the gay community.

Much has been achieved in recent years in order to reverse this tragic caricature. Christian involvement in education, training and prevention programmes, coupled with tender care and understanding for the sick and dying, has done a great deal to remove that impression. Images of a cosy, self-righteous, gloating rejection of AIDS sufferers are being replaced by a compassionate benevolence.

While, in one sense, many instances of AIDS do reflect a kind of horribly 'poetic' justice, AIDS is far from God's intention or desire for humankind. The simple fact remains that God has designed us as sexual beings to express that sexuality in a heterosexual relationship within the context of a lifelong commitment in marriage. To ignore his mandate and intention is to place ourselves at the mercy of the forces of evil.

God's justice is not seen in the punishment that he metes out to offenders, rather in 'giving us up' to reap the bitter harvest of the ungodly seed we have sown (Rom 1:26). In saying that, our 'wild oats' do not place us beyond the scope of his forgiveness. Far from it; but we do suffer consequences that he would never have wished, but which result from our choice alone.

The results do not merely affect ourselves, for this plague

spreads. The 'innocent' recipients of AIDS by such means as blood transfusion, also deserve our love, care and respect, for human sin wreaks havoc upon all our lives.

I drive a diesel-powered car. If, of my own volition, I determine to fill the tank with petrol, rather than diesel, I will suffer the inevitable consequences. The car will stop, and the engine will be severely damaged. Is this to be regarded as the judgement of God, or the logical by-product of human foolishness?

Ignoring the Maker's instructions

To ignore the manufacturer's handbook, and the maker's instructions, is to render myself liable to face the inevitable results.

God has revealed his plan and purpose for humankind in Scripture. He has told us how to live. If we reject 'the best' that he has planned for us, then disaster will follow. Our sinful disobedience will ultimately produce tragic results beyond ourselves, for to play into the hands of the Evil One makes it certain that the innocent will also suffer.

It is legitimate to suggest that God should never have given us the capacity to choose in the first place. But in that case we would be reduced to the level of reluctant robots programmed to choose the good. The potential for that was shattered in the Garden of Eden when our spiritual ancestors exercised the freedom God offered them in order to reject his instructions and manufacture their own plan for life. The consequences of self-willed disobedience are no less tragic today.

Where can truth be found?

Our world has long engaged in a search for truth. Ultimately two options emerge – either to discover truth within ourselves, or to discover it in God himself. If there is a Creator, then truth originated with him; if not, then we are left alone in the universe to discover what works for us.

'Religious humanists regard the universe as self-existing and not created. Humanism asserts that the nature of the universe depicted by modern science makes unacceptable any supernatural or cosmic guarantees of human values' (Paul Kurtz, ed. *Humanist Manifesto I & II* [Prometheus Books: New York,

1973]). The Christian view is at variance with this, for it sees God as the author of truth and therefore 'All moral obligation resolves itself into the obligation of conformity to the will of God' (Charles Hodge, *Systematic Theology* [Thomas Nelson: London and Edinburgh, 1873]).

For Christians the search for truth begins, not in ourselves, but in a Garden. It was there that God established his creation ordinances for humankind. The nature of work, responsibility for the environment, accountability to God, and the complementary relationship between men and women were introduced as the basic principles for living in God's world.

Human disobedience resulted in the loss of paradise. Perfect truth and harmony were replaced by death, destruction, hatred, toil and disorder. Our own self-will and self-interest won: obedience to the truth was lost, and the unique relationship between men, women and God was shattered.

God's truth may have been rejected, but it could never be destroyed, for God chose Israel as his people to live in accordance with his truth. The plan God had for his people was revealed in his covenant agreements and through his laws. *Truth and the people of Israel*

The nature of God's truth is vividly illustrated by the principles of justice contained in the covenants. The people of Israel were to treat each other fairly (Lev 25:17), and honestly (Lev 19:36; Amos 8:4-7). Widows, orphans, slaves and strangers were to be given special treatment (Ex 22:21-24; Lev 19:33-34; Deut 15:12). Those who were disadvantaged were to receive help and support (Lev 25:35, 39-41).

Israel was to live in obedience to God's requirements and would inherit his favour in the Promised Land. His truth demanded that they reject occult practices and false gods (Ex 34:17; Lev 19:26; 26:1).

Whenever God's people rebelled against his truth, rejecting the principles of social justice and compassion, and pursued other gods, then the prophets were sent to uphold God's truth. They denounced injustice and the mistreatment of the powerless (Amos 2:6; 5:12; Micah 6:11); they repudiated narrow-minded nationalism (Amos 9:7); and the abuse of wealth and power (Is 5:7,23; Micah 2:8-9; Zeph 3:3). Their message was essentially that true religion and respect for the truth must walk hand in hand (Micah 6:6-8; Jer 6:19-20).

On Mount Sinai God gave Moses the Ten Commandments which set the same high standard of moral, ethical and spiritual purity for all Israel (Ex 20:2-17). This law was to form the basis for the wide-ranging system of moral and civil laws which were to govern Jewish society. God always intended that his people should live by his truth.

Truth expressed by Jesus   Truth received its fullest expression in a divine personality. Uniquely, Jesus embodied the truth of God, and his message was different from any that had been heard before. While the law had dealt with actions, Jesus challenged the character and motives of each individual.

* He condemned moral blindness, callousness and pride (Mt 7:3; Mk 3:5; Lk 18:9).

* Jesus denounced those who committed murder and adultery in their hearts, even if it did not surface in their actions (Mt 5:21-22,28).

* He cut across the racial convictions of so many of his contemporaries (Lk 10:33; Mt 8:10-12).

* Jesus affirmed both women and children (Mt 19:14; Jn 4:7-26).

* He challenged the desire to accumulate wealth and power (Mt 6:19-34; Mk 4:18-19; Lk 12:15; 21:1-4).

* Jesus advocated a neighbour-love which operated with no conditions or requirements on the part of the recipient, even extending it to our enemies (Lk 6:32-36; 14:12-14).

Supremely, in the Sermon on the Mount, Jesus demanded higher standards from his followers in relation to issues like murder, adultery, oaths, revenge, divorce, reconciliation, remarriage and the hatred of their enemies (Mt 5:21-48). Religious leaders were not to be guilty of a special-case mentality in relation to the truth of God. In fact they had to amend their behaviour concerning their hypocritical attitudes, prayer lives, fasting and public giving (Mt 6:1-18).

The words of Jesus were designed to give his listeners a new insight into the truth of God.

Here is a Christian value system, ethical standard, religious devotion, attitude to money, ambition, lifestyle and network of relationships – all of which are totally at variance with those of the non-Christian world. And this Christian counter-culture is the life of the kingdom of God, a fully human life indeed, but lived out under the divine rule' (John Stott, *Message of the Sermon on the Mount* [IVP: Leicester, 1978]).

Finally, truth was to be found in the pages of Scripture. The early church took the words of Jesus and the apostolic teaching seriously. The Holy Spirit breathed the authority of God into its pages so that today all can be aware of the way in which God intends people to live within his world (2 Tim 3:16-17).

How can I be sure?

Every society needs the rule of law. The question arises as to what foundation is required for laws to be created.

The Christian answer is straightforward – biblical commands reveal the will of God. The knowledge of right and wrong does not come through philosophical speculation, but by simple obedience to God's law (1 Sam 15:22; Rom 2:18). Laws based upon the Ten Commandments will therefore reflect God's desires rather than human self-interest or ingenuity.

* Biblical ethical standards represent God's truth declared for his creation. They are designed for our benefit because they came from the One who knows and loves his people personally. Where a society has chosen another foundation, disaster has been the inevitable result. The German Third Reich is a good instance. Denial of God's law and perversion of its standards resulted in the annihilation of millions and the demise of an empire.

* Biblical commands demand a higher standard. No human code has ever surpassed the biblical demand that we love and imitate God (Lev 11:44; Lk 6:36; Eph 5:1-2). However, to live in this way requires Christian conviction. For it is impossible to please God apart from the Holy Spirit's energising of the believer (Gal 5:16-18, 22-23). Throughout the pages of Scripture ethical conclusions are only drawn from initial statements of theological truth (Ex 20:2; Mt 5:43-48; 1 Cor 6:12-20).

Whenever society deserts God's law, the results can be seen in

The results of deserting God's law both private and public morality. The initial cracks are witnessed when public servants are disclosed as living in a way that society regards as morally reprehensible.

Politicians are particularly sensitive about accusations of 'sleaze'. They often insist that their private morality has nothing to do with their public service. The inconsistency of this approach is obvious to every impartial observer. For why should we be prepared to believe anything that a person says if they are prepared to lie to their wife or husband, children or colleagues?

Negative actions towards others are always acts against God (Mt 25:45). When a person's heart is corrupt, it will show through their words and actions (Mt 5:17-20). The fact remains that private behaviour which breaks God's laws and tarnishes an individual's moral character, often makes them a less valued member of society. The world becomes a poorer place because of the manner in which people conduct their private affairs.

Public disillusionment is the inevitable result, because private morality is the essential foundation on which public trust is built.

If this is true of the Royal Family, politicians, civil servants and media personalities, it is also true of church leaders. We commend the gospel by the way that we live, and while all of us acknowledge our failures in this respect, we must also acknowledge the responsibility that we all bear.

We should not be surprised that society remembers its Judaeo-Christian heritage. Non-Christians maintain high expectations of the lifestyle of Christians and possess an innate conviction about God's universal moral laws (Rom 2:1, 12-13, 23).

Part of our human nature is our conscience. Being made in God's image we retain an innate sense of right and wrong (Rom 2:12-16). The continuing demand of God's truth is that we act in obedience to his teachings in Scripture and his promptings within our hearts and lives. For truth is not just to be learned or recognised, it is to be lived and obeyed!

6

Grace and Truth

How can we express the truth in love? The central theme of this chapter is that grace and truth must always walk together. Truth is not merely a set of rules, but a living out of God's steadfast love. We need to live in the constant knowledge that God has taken the initiative in loving us – and that we in turn must take the initiative in communicating his truth to others.

Grace and Truth

"Nothing conquers except truth: the victory of truth is charity'.

Augustine

Dressed in an immaculate dark grey suit, his black shoes spotless, and hair well greased back, the figure was imposing. With index finger raised, the voice of Protestant orthodoxy boomed out his pronouncements through raised megaphone. The message was condemning, judgemental and to the point, laced with quotations from the Authorised Version. The handful of listeners were left in no doubt as to their eternal destination.

At the same moment, many miles away, TV cameras were trained on the crumpled suit and ruffled hair of a nervously smiling clergyman. Loved by his mining parishioners with whom he had once stood on the picket line, he explained that the love of God could be discovered in every religion, even Christianity.

Clutching his handkerchief he mopped his brow as he recounted the story of Muslims, Sikhs, Buddhists and Christians engaging in inter-faith prayers in his church for world peace. This expression of tolerance and partnership had filled the church for the first time in many years.

There is a certain sense of predictability in these two caricatures. On the one hand, the endearing compassion of the cleric whose character obscures the emptiness of his church and the betrayal of his message. For him the rejection of orthodox doctrines relating to the Virgin Birth, miracles, bodily resurrection of Jesus and Scripture is automatic. Yet his personal warmth, courtesy and kindness make him impossible to dislike.

By contrast, the intrinsic bitterness and hostility of the pedant who wears his bigotry on his sleeve make him difficult to live with – and impossible to like. The harshness of the messenger obscures the intrinsic relevance and truth of the message he proclaims.

Yet this is only half the truth. Media stereotypes disguise reality. Many would be amazed to discover the genuine article – the truth behind the public persona. It may be hard to believe, but the strident voice and bombastic aggression hid a compassionate and caring man who consistently pastored his people. As for the public face of doubt – behind it lurked a genuine faith and a heartfelt commitment to encouraging people to believe in the Christ he had found to be true.

In one case the messenger obscured the message, in the other the reverse was true. The simple fact is that conviction and lifestyle, content and presentation need to walk hand in hand. The tragedy is that nowadays one rarely finds the consistency in truth and character which Jesus urged on his followers.

A close personal friend is a Government minister and was brave enough to write the Foreword to this book. A few years ago he held a position in the Northern Ireland office and invited me to speak to a number of church leaders from the province at Stormont Castle.

As we chatted together before the meeting he came out with a statement that I will probably never forget. As an assessment of the spiritual dilemma that each one of us faces it stands as a masterly description. 'I read in scripture,' he said, 'of a man named Jesus who was full of grace and truth. Sometimes I see church leaders who have more truth than grace. On other occasions I meet those who have more grace than truth. It seems to me that the church will never recover until we have both in equal measure.' That is a devastating analysis. Too often we have concentrated on one at the expense of the other. The two must always exist in combination together.

It can never be sufficient to exhibit love, *Grace and truth* compassion and generosity of spirit at the expense of *in balance* the truth of the message we should proclaim. Nor can we ever excuse our deficiencies of lifestyle by the truth of our pronouncements. If we know the truth we must live in a manner worthy of it – and if we are to live Godly lives, we cannot avoid our obligation to boldly declare the whole message of Christ. For grace and truth must always walk together. Neither can ever be sacrificed for the other.

The truth of God

The teaching of Jesus evoked the admiration of the crowds as they listened. The humour of the parables must have made them laugh. The profound way in which he summarised the entire Jewish law, 'Love your neighbour as yourself' (Lk 10:27), stunned the opposition. The people were constantly amazed at what he said (Mt 7:28). But then he announced that truth was not only what he said, but who he was – and that must have taken their breath away (Jn 14:6).

The full nature of the shock presented by this announcement of Jesus can only be properly appreciated by examining the nature of truth as it appeared to Jewish eyes.

The Old Testament did speak of 'truth', as opposed to falsehood, in terms of facts which could be established as being correct (Ex 18:21; Deut 13:14; 17:4; 1 Kings 10:6). In this sense Jesus proclaimed that he was utterly trustworthy and reliable. No-one need entertain any doubts about him. It is significant to note that the Old Testament thinks more of the basis of truth in a reliable person than in the mere facts of a case.

Truth is seen as the attribute of a person (Gen 42:16), and is supremely a distinctive characteristic of God (Ps 25:10; 31:5; Jer 10:10). He is truth (Heb: *'emet̲, 'emûnâ*) and the word denotes consistency and faithfulness (Deut 32:4; Hos 2:20). Unlike the capriciousness of pagan deities, God is unchanging in his truth which even 'reaches to the clouds' (Ps 108:4).

As he is truth, then so is his word (Ps 119:89) and his

judgement and transmission of truth (Ps 57:3; 96:13). The whole picture is one of stability, unflinching justice, firmness and reliability. If this were to seem too impassive or remote, *'emet* is frequently used in conjunction with *hesed*, pronounced 'chesed'

God's steadfast love and meaning 'steadfast love' (Ps 57:3; 108:4), and in this sense 'mercy and truth are met together' (Ps 85:10 AV). God declares his love to Moses and announces that he is worthy of confidence, but then declares that this demands integrity, for his people must live in obedience to his commands (Ex 34:6-7).

This truth is therefore no mere abstract theory located in some timeless zone outside human history. It is here and now, relating to actions as well as words. Indeed, for a God of truth, and for those who would seek to follow him, word and deed become the same thing. God has spoken, he is reliable, so it must happen. Because of his faithfulness we can trust his truth, it never fails.

So the statements of Jesus are amazing. He is proclaiming that he is faithful, reliable, full of love and his word is not to be doubted. He is to be obeyed because he is always correct and can never be less than true to his people. We can have total confidence in him for he is *the* truth, he is God himself.

The far-reaching implications of this were obvious. To reject Jesus was to reject his Father as well! So if one wanted to find truth, then the answer was simply to search for, and then follow, Jesus.

When Jesus insists that he is speaking the truth (Lk 4:25; 9:27; 12:44), he is declaring the full, real and absolute state of affairs. The Greek word *alētheia* and its derivatives express this precise intellectual meaning. The sense is therefore of that which is not false or short-changing the listener, but real and complete.

Jesus is therefore continually insisting that his hearers do not need to doubt his words. They reflect the full counsel of God (Mk 5:33).

The adjective *alēthinos* often carries the idea, previously introduced by Plato, of something real as opposed to an illusion or a mere resemblance or copy. Plato insisted that 'God is true in deed and word', and neither changes himself nor deceives others.

Like the earlier Greek philosopher, Pormenides, he enquired as to the nature of real being and drew a contrast between the way of truth and the way of seeming. Truth is reality and truth cannot change. For Jesus to describe himself as truth was to prepare the way for the description of him as 'the same yesterday, and today, and for ever' (Heb 13:8).

In this way Scripture announces that reality is found in Jesus, not in the prefiguring of his work and ministry in Old Testament rituals. *The reality of Jesus*

* Jesus is the true bread and the true vine (Jn 6:32, 15:1). He is the eternal reality symbolised by bread and wine (Mk 14:22-24; Lk 22:19-20).

* Jesus introduces real worship in spirit and truth, not just the sincere rituals practised in Jerusalem or on Mount Gerazim (Jn 4:21-23). He establishes worship in both spirit and truth.

* Jesus is the minister of the true tabernacle, as opposed to the shadowy reflection of the Levitical ritual (Heb 8:3-6).

Similarly *alētheia* affirms that Jesus carries and mediates the truth (Jn 1:17). The Holy Spirit can then lead men and women into that reality. The disciples of Jesus can enter into the truth of new birth (Jn 3:3-5; Jas 2:18). They can:

* Know the truth (Jn 8:32; 2 Jn:1).
* Do the truth (Jn 3:21).
* Live and remain in the truth (Jn 8:44).

For this reason the apostle Paul believed in the truth. He saw that to encounter the truth as it is found in Jesus will result in a transformed life, where the believer has turned away from his old deceitful habits (Eph 4:21-22). *Paul's view of truth*

He saw truth as an essential part of the Christian's defences against attack from the enemy (Eph 6:14). Paul believed that the gospel had nothing to fear from the truth, openness to the truth would only enhance the Christian cause (2 Cor 13:8).

He believed in the power of the truth. It symbolises new life (1 Cor 5:8; Eph 4:25), exposes lies (Rom 3:4), and can even be the means of leading someone to salvation (2 Thess 2:10).

All this because Jesus inaugurated the reign of truth and is the personification of it (Jn 14:6). He, uniquely, is *the* truth. In him can be found all that one needs to know about God, creation and humankind.

Some biblical scholars have concentrated on highlighting the differences between Old and New Testament meanings of truth. They are therefore contrasting 'faithfulness' with 'reality'. However, the Old Testament meaning is occasionally carried over into the New. Ideas of dependability, truthfulness and integrity are applied to God (Rom 3:7, 15:8), and to people (2 Cor 7:14; Eph 5:9). The thought of a God who can be trusted is implicit throughout the New Testament, because Jesus is the author and content of truth.

This truth is more than a credal formula. Jesus is the *logos,* the creative Word of God, emanating from the Father (Jn 1:1). He is God's active word, he is the truth, and God's revelation of his truth must be observed and obeyed.

While the Greek view saw truth as just a pale reflection of the ideal and eternal concept of truth, the Jewish concept of truth was always dynamic. Truth lives, and can never exist as merely an idea, it has to have a living expression. That is the idea behind James' assertion that faith without works is dead. In Jesus truth was put into practice.

Rules are not enough

Christianity has often been regarded as a system of rules and regulations by which its adherents are supposed to live. Popular opinion suggests that any future destiny would be determined by a set of scales on which our good deeds must outweigh our bad ones.

It is true that Jesus called for obedience – but not just to a string of rules. It is therefore not surprising to see him attacking the hypocrisy of the Pharisees (Mt 23:2-3, 23-24; Lk 11:46). They had reduced the great truth of God to slavish obedience to a set of propositions.

The Jewish concept of God's law   The scribes and Pharisees regarded the Law as being divine because it contained God's last word about everything. If a situation was not dealt with explicitly, then it must be implicit in the Law, for this contained the very truth of God.

After their return from exile the Jewish rabbis taught their people to show great regard for the truth and requirements of God. They saw this revealed in the Torah, which combined the written law of the Ten Commandments with an oral law, and which tradition claimed was revealed by God to Moses on Mount Sinai.

The oral law consisted of 613 further rules (*mitzvot*), of which 248 were positive and 365 negative requirements. These were regarded as obligatory for all of God's people.

A new group emerged to spearhead a radical return to the law. They worked out the detailed implications of each rule and regulation – they were the scribes. Their counterparts were the Pharisees, whose name means 'The Separate Ones'. They divorced themselves from the ordinary activities of life in order to devote themselves fully to the task of living out these requirements.

The scribes reduced the great principles of the Law to thousands upon thousands of regulations. Scribal law was finally codified in written form during the third century AD. This volume, the Mishnah, would run into eight hundred pages in English. Later, commentaries were produced to explain the Mishnah, and one of these – the Babylonian Talmud – consists of sixty printed volumes. Keeping the will of God was clearly a full-time occupation! This was regarded as the totality of God's truth, and it must be obeyed.

One regulation was to do no work on the Sabbath. Scribal law laid down that to carry a burden was to work, but what was a burden? This was defined as, 'food equal to the weight of a dried fig, enough wine for mixing in a goblet, milk enough for one swallow, honey enough to put upon a wound, oil enough to anoint someone, water enough to moisten an eye-salve... ink enough to write two letters of the alphabet...' etc, etc.

Scribes spent hours in argument over whether a woman might wear a brooch or wig – was that work? Could a man lift his child on the Sabbath – was that work? Did a tailor commit sin by inadvertently going out with a needle stuck in his robe – was that work?

Some things were permitted. Medical practice was allowed to take place on the Sabbath if a life was at stake. However, this was limited to preventing further deterioration in the patient's condition. It is little wonder that Jesus created consternation when he healed people completely instead of just arresting their decline.

Religion and the will of God was reduced to a legalism of petty rules and regulations. The Old Testament itself contains few such directives. In its pages we discover God's principles which, under his guidance, he wanted people to apply to the individual situations of life.

Jesus provides a fresh understanding of the law
Jesus burst onto this scene of conventional Judaism with a very different view of the will of God. Instead of obedience to a host of rules and regulations, added by human tradition to the Ten Commandments which God had given, he demanded a more positive adherence to the will of God. Jesus boldly announced that he had not come to destroy the law, but to fulfil it (Mt 5:17). The righteousness exhibited by his followers was to exceed that of the Pharisees (Mt 5:20).

Jesus rejected this oral scribal law. God had never required this kind of minute observance of ridiculously detailed instructions. Instead Jesus revealed a new understanding of God's truth – forgiveness, salvation and freedom.

The Law contained in the Prophets and the Pentateuch was to be fulfilled in Jesus (Mt 5:17). Now his people could live, 'not under the law, but under grace' (Rom 6:14-15). So Paul could proclaim that 'Christ is the end of the law' (Rom 10:4): he had replaced it!

The nature of grace
Grace has been defined as 'the unmerited favour of God'. It is therefore closely allied to the Old Testament concept of steadfast love, in Hebrew, *hesed*. Luther translated this word as 'gnade', the German word for grace. However, the two are not the same, for steadfast love can denote a mutual relationship between God and man. Grace is strictly one way, it is God's love towards us.

Grace is therefore linked to God's 'favour'. This carries the sense of the irrelevance of any merit on our part in the sight of God, for none of us can ever do him a favour! Grace is what we receive from him, and none of us can ever deserve it!

Grace is discovered in the Law itself, for Israel's election by God to be his people is attributed to God's free choice, rather than to any righteousness on the part of Israel (Deut 7:7-8). God is always at work in taking the initiative towards his people – that is grace.

If, as individuals, we are to change our lives, it can never be by human effort, but only by the grace of God. He alone can put a new heart within us (Ezek 36:26).

The New Testament sharply contrasts the two principles of law and grace (Jn 1:17). God's *charis*, the Greek word for grace, is used by Jesus in this sense for the first time. This concept is introduced into the world by Jesus (Tit 2:11). His *agape*, love is the gratuitous love of Jesus towards us, and he alone can give us the power to live a moral life. This dynamic sense of God's grace being evidenced in our fearless courage and effective witness for him is seen in the life of the early church (Acts 4:33).

For Paul, this principle, of grace achieving in us that which the law could never do, lay at the heart of his message. We are sinners, but are justified, made right with God – not through human effort – but his grace alone (Rom 3:21–4:25). God, in his grace, therefore treats us as if we had never sinned.

Peter continued this theme by speaking of 'the grace of life' and the promise of future glory (1 Pet 3:7; 5:10).

Scripture presents us with a vivid comparison between human struggle and efforts portrayed by Israel's failure to obey the law, and God's grace in Christ which alone could bring people to himself.

This is the very heartbeat of the Christian message, for it is the truth of Christ reflecting the character of God himself. Our message is one that transcends words alone, for God's truth is demonstrated in the lives that his grace empowers us to live.

Not by words alone

Jesus was never prepared to hide behind his words, nor was he prepared to tolerate those who attempted to conceal their actions behind smokescreens of fine words. Such people he exposed with unsparing scorn. Jesus knew what lay hidden in human hearts.

His piercing gaze penetrated the true motives of all those he met. Jesus rejected any discrepancy between word and deed, or statement and reality. He knew where such things came from, for their source was Satan himself.

Jesus never failed to match his words by his deeds. When he proclaimed grace to the outcast, he proceeded to dine with tax collectors and sinners. He announced that the kingdom was nearby, and then inaugurated it upon a cross. For Jesus the message was to be both spoken and lived; to sacrifice one for the sake of the other would have been an intolerable inconsistency.

This stands in stark contrast to our society today, for we live in a world that is full of words. Dialogue, argument, gossip, criticism, chatter, debate or conversation – society seems never to be short of comment.

The result is often that we become reluctant 'to believe our ears' and require more evidence than mere verbal argument. As Eliza Doolittle plaintively sang in *My Fair Lady*:

> Words, words, words,
> I'm sick of words.
> Sing me no song,
> Read me no rhyme.
> Don't waste my time,
> Show me.

Disillusioned with the emptiness of a plethora of mere words, we desire to see truth in action.

Truth does not need to be demonstrated in order for it to be true. Truth remains true whether we recognise it or not. However, while acting out the truth can never alter its nature or status as being that which is true, it does make people more able to believe it.

Truth is not abstract
Truth, by definition, must be true. Yet God never created truth to exist as a mere abstract concept. He always intended that it should be recognised and identified. It was for that reason he sent Jesus as the living embodiment of truth. For truth is not abstract, it is living and breathing. Truth walked this earth in the person of Jesus.

Similarly, we have to conclude that truth is meant to be passed on to others. In order to convey truth, there will be times when words are not enough. Our contemporary consumer society responds to observable results. So truth is not just there to be believed, we need to live in the light of that truth. We need to demonstrate the grace of God. Therefore each of us needs to live in a manner that actively commends the truth about God to other people.

Many stories have been told about the life and works of Francis of Assisi. Some owe their genesis to popular mythology, but interestingly the facts of his life surpass tales told about him. Francis repented of his years as a prodigal, indulging his own sensual appetites, and devoted his life to the service of God. He was a missionary at heart. His saintly life – though not all his reported theological pronouncements – earn our admiration and esteem.

An example: Francis of Assisi

During the fifth crusade, in 1219, Francis appeared at the court of the Sultan of Egypt. He was totally convinced that military force was not the means by which to conquer Islam. Francis preached the message of Jesus with courage and boldness before the Sultan. It was not just his words that won him a respectful hearing. By arriving as a defenceless man in shabby clothing, and a lifestyle marked by piety and poverty he earned the opportunity to speak.

The decisive factor was his personal holiness rather than his eloquence, for our deeds so often speak louder than our words.

If we are truly to be witnesses to the truth of the gospel then we must never be content merely to announce the good news, we must be living demonstrations of its reality.

Every individual Christian has a God-given calling to both declare and live the truth. Churches and fellowships can never be content with merely proclaiming truth while confined within the cosy ecclesiastical insulation of a building. We are under divine instructions to invade our communities with the love of God.

Words of themselves can never be enough. The truth needs to be caught as well as taught. It is to be practised as well as believed. When this happens we will discover that truth is both infectious and contagious. Carried by lives that bear vivid testimony to the truth in our words, it spreads like wildfire!

We must therefore live as witnesses to the truth. This will affect every aspect and sphere of our human existence. Truth liberates, convicts, empowers and challenges. It must mould our lives so that we faithfully carry its message to the ends of the earth – we can never rely on words alone.

Too good to be true

Most Christians feel comfortable with this emphasis. We recognise that we need to live the Christian life in an appropriate manner, and that when we fail forgiveness is available in Jesus Christ.

Declaring the truth

This is a comforting reality. Our stumbling-block comes when we realise that truth needs to be declared as well as lived. For the message of Jesus was, and is, an uncompromising one. He announced that he alone was the truth about God; that is the uncomfortable message that we are called upon to proclaim.

This kind of assertion sounds strange to secular ears. We have become conditioned to believe that tolerance of all perspectives, rather than exclusive claims, represents the highest virtue. It is argued that it must be good and right to accept each person, attitude or belief as being equally valid and true. Few would doubt that this is a proper 'Christian' conviction. Yet this concept is miles removed from the unique claims which Jesus presented for himself.

In this he echoed his Father. God has always demanded the exclusive obedience of his people. He has issued divine commands and, because he is perfect, his instructions must be just and right. Nor are they just designed for Christians. We worship a Creator God who reveals the way that all people should live. As Roger Forster has succinctly observed, 'If you want to live in God's world, you ought to live in it God's way'.

Such assertions are guaranteed to be unpopular. They smack of bigotry and intransigence, of Christians imposing their will on everybody else. We need to avoid giving the impression of recreating the Inquisition and attempting to enforce our own perspective. We may seem to be making an arrogant suggestion. But Christianity does claim to be *the* truth from God for all humankind.

This Christian conviction often seems to protest that it is too rigid and authoritarian. The question is asked as to how one rule can apply to all people, and to every situation? That would constitute a fair objection if it were not for two important factors:

(i) Christian truth is committed to the fact that it is not a human being laying down this direction, but an all-knowing God.

(ii) This same God is the Creator; as such he is concerned for the totality of his creation. His intention is benevolent, in other words, he is uniquely positioned to save us from ourselves.

The heart of Christianity does not lie in the tolerance of every person's understanding of truth, but in recognising what is true, and what is false. Similarly, human freedom is not to be formed in an equal acceptance of all viewpoints, but by embracing the truth of Jesus Christ (Jn 8:32, 36).

This does not mean that we should ever persecute those who disagree with us. The history of the church is littered with examples of intolerance that should never have been. Instead our duty lies in maintaining the truth by living according to biblical standards and proclaiming the divine alternative that Jesus proclaimed to all who are prepared to listen.

Unlike Islamic fundamentalists, we are not commanded to inflict our standards upon a reluctant society. Christianity has no place for the sword in spreading its rule or establishing orthodoxy. It is the persuasiveness of our lives that must provide the living demonstration of the truth of our message.

This should never be used as an excuse for not entering into debate with those with whom we disagree. It has been common for Christians to be *Being willing to confront* frightened at the thought of confrontation. This should not be the case!

Far from resisting confrontations, these can present a genuine opportunity to share the truth of our faith. If we really believe that Jesus is the truth, then we need never fear the consequences of exposing that truth in public debate. It is for that reason I enjoy working within the secular media, for differences of opinion are a regular feature, and disagreement makes an interesting programme. Christians may not win each argument, but we have no right to conceal the truth among ourselves.

For too long we have been content to hide away in our own privatised ghetto. While boldly proclaiming our message from church pulpits, we have been sadly reluctant to expose Christian truth to a wider audience.

The time has come to change. With evangelical Christians

making up nearly 50% of Protestant churchgoers, they have a voice – and need to make it heard! Public opinion will not always be on our side, but as the Quaker, William Penn, aptly put it, 'Right is right, even if everyone is against it; and wrong is wrong, even if everyone is for it.'

This will mean being prepared to argue our case logically, to speak the truth, clearly and carefully, and not to be too disheartened by those who choose to disagree with us!

Truth and grace can be friends

Nowhere was this more clearly illustrated than in the person of Jesus (Jn 1:14). The glory of God was revealed as being full of grace and truth. God's glory is his supreme goodness, and in Jesus integrity and compassion walked hand in hand.

This reflected the time that Moses stood on Mount Sinai and God's goodness passed before him, and God proclaimed his name (Ex 33:19). The character of God and the truth of God will always travel together, as they did in Jesus. The point in John's Gospel is therefore a simple one – to 'see' God is nothing less than observing his glory in Jesus Christ.

The exciting reality is that Jesus did claim to be the truth about God, and his actions amplified and confirmed his words. Many who have begun by seeking to qualify his statements about himself, have ended up entranced by the glorious wonder of their truthfulness.

For the Christian the biblical picture of Jesus is no idealised portrait of a stained-glass saint. It is an honest description of the only person in history whose actions and words were totally consistent with each other. For Jesus his theories were simple statements of fact. For us the conclusion is that truth begins and ends with Jesus. In Jesus grace and truth were uniquely conjoined. When he comes to our lives it is to introduce the same change in us.

One nineteenth-century Cornish clergyman, William Haslam, was preaching on the Pharisees and their attempt to live by the law of God. He realised that he was as much a failure as they had been. While he preached he turned his life over to Jesus Christ and felt light and joy enter his soul. His face portrayed what was happening and a cry went up from the congregation, 'The parson is converted!'.

7

Marooned in a Minefield

How should Christians regard those of other religions – as people with whom we can profitably hold a dialogue? Or should we go further and attempt to win them for Christ? In this chapter we look at the difficult question of other world faiths and the nature of conversion.

Marooned in a Minefield

*Magna est veritas, et praevalet. Great is truth
and it prevails.*

Apocrypha, 1 Esdras 4:41

The Albigensians were a medieval sect who flourished in
southern France during the twelfth and thirteenth centuries. They
believed in two gods – the bad god of the Old Testament who
imprisoned the human soul in a physical body, and Christ the Son
of a good God who had no real body but came to release our
spirits from this evil material world.

They accepted the New Testament and many Christian doctrines,
but rejected the humanity of Jesus, the incarnation and the
sacraments, because they completely separated spirit and matter.

The difficulty for the church lay in the popularity of this group.
Their humble, disciplined lifestyle contrasted vividly with the
materialism, luxury and abuses of the contemporary church.

The answer to the problem swiftly emerged in the person of
Simon of Montfort, a French nobleman who was Earl of
Leicester. Instead of employing spiritual arguments or gentle
reason, he simply began to wipe out the Albigensians.

The methods he employed were savage – even by the standards

of those brutal days. Entering one castle he gouged out the eyes of one hundred men, and cut off their noses and upper lips. On another occasion he entered a house containing one hundred and forty men and women, and 'since he was a Catholic man and wished them all to be saved and come to recognise the truth, he first urged them to convert to the Catholic faith. But having no success, he had them dragged out... a huge fire was kindled and they were all thrown into it' (ed. Elizabeth Hallam, *Chronicles of the Crusades* [Weidenfeld & Nicolson: New York, 1989]).

Simon had no doubt that he was furthering the cause of God and that his was a legitimate Crusade. The epitaph on his tomb at Carcassonne depicted him as a saint and martyr.

After his death one damning verdict on his life was recorded,

> If one may seek Christ by killing men and shedding blood, by winning lands by violence, by fostering evil and snuffing out good, and by slaughtering women and children, then must Simon surely shine resplendent in heaven. (William of Tudela, *Chanson de la Croisade contre les Albigeois* [Paris, 1960]).

Such atrocities have not been confined to any particular faith or period of history. The intransigence of Islamic fundamentalists and the horrors of Nazi Germany present vivid reminders of the ever-present dangers of intolerance.

It is perhaps unsurprising to record that toleration has come to be regarded in much of society as a higher virtue than truth. We have been encouraged to accept all ideas and opinions as equally valid. In order to avoid accusations of extremism or bigotry, we avoid passing judgement on the beliefs of anyone else.

As Christians we are faced with a serious dilemma. We abhor all forms of persecution, yet we can never confuse tolerance with compromise. We must always echo the words of Martin Luther, 'Here I stand'. We can do no less today. For religious conviction is not redundant – people are still searching for truth.

Faith for today?

At the dawning of the twentieth century it was already being confidently predicted that humankind was rapidly outgrowing its need for God. The concepts that 'God is dead', and that humanity had 'come of age', removed the necessity for religious belief. No longer would spiritual convictions possess significance in a materialistic age.

As the century progressed, a growing secularisation permeated much of Western Europe. Religious belief came to be greeted with general apathy or indifference as it was replaced by secular thinking and values. However, the rapid advance of atheism has been arrested by the fall of communism. More recently 'futurologists' have pointed to a renaissance of spiritual convictions. They see this 'religious revival' as a general phenomenon, not limited to any particular faith.

Far from faith dying out, the evidence of recent studies indicates that it remains alive and well, even in Western Europe. A survey by researchers at Chicago University in 1992 showed that in Britain nearly seventy percent maintained a belief in God, a *Religion remains alive, even in Western Europe* figure confirmed by the 1993 European Values Group Survey. The Chicago study also confirmed that fifty percent of those they interviewed believed in life after death, and nearly a fifth claimed to attend church two or three times a month and prayed daily.

It is interesting to note from the parallel European study that more people in Britain stated they believed in heaven than in life after death. It demonstrated that people, 'elect to hold beliefs that allow them to have their cake and eat it too' (*New Statesman and Society*, August, 1993).

The author of the Chicago report, Professor Andrew Greeley, insists that the survey shows that religion not only persists in its importance to people – it actually matters. He argues that religious faith and devotion, as measured by personal convictions and frequency of prayer, still have an impact on how people view issues of truth and social legislation. These include concern for the poor, opposition to the death penalty, and the search for personal happiness. He concluded that 'It is the reverse of everything that the theories of secularisation and religious doctrine lead us to anticipate. God is not dead, he is alive and well, even in Britain' (*The Times,* May 19th, 1993).

These convictions are not limited to Christianity. Technology

A range of religious options has now introduced us to a wider world. The development of the media has made us increasingly aware that we live in a world that grows smaller each day. Locked up in our global village we have become far more aware of alternative religious beliefs to Christianity.

Meanwhile the influx of other ethnic groupings into British society has radically altered public perspectives. No longer does 'religion' mean Christianity alone, for over five per cent of the UK population are adherents of other faiths. A half of this number are Muslims, with Sikhs as the next largest group. No longer is it enough only to consider our own religious tradition, we are forced to recognise the existence, in close proximity, of other major world religions.

Living in a South London street can produce its own complications. A Muslim up the road, a Hindu family down the road, Buddhists and Sikhs around the corner, Catholics and Protestants in alternate houses – then the Jehovah's Witnesses knocking at the door, while Mormons are visiting in the next street. When it comes to religion there is little shortage of choice!

Presented with this kaleidoscope of belief, it is unsurprising that many confess to a slight case of confusion.

Confronted by such a huge variety of religious options it has become easy to suggest that everyone is entitled to make their own choice. Therefore, surely, no single faith should be allowed to assume that it alone represents truth?

Should Christians accept a pluralistic worldview? This has been the conclusion of our contemporary society. Its verdict is that, as Britain, Australia, the USA and many others are now multi-faith societies, so the church needs to open up the way for shared religious worship, especially on civic and state occasions. Any other attitude would be to maintain that Christianity has a monopoly on truth, and this would open us all to charges of bigotry and intolerance.

It has been argued that every faith has emerged from its own culture and tradition and is therefore as valid as any other. The best way forward for modern society must, therefore, lie in the encouragement of each other's beliefs. TV personality Anne Diamond arrived at the ultimate statement of this tendency when she declared 'It doesn't matter what you believe, just as long as you are sincere about it.'

Truth is therefore reduced to the level of personal individual conviction and the sincerity with which it is held. The results of this viewpoint are quite devastating. While it appeals to our sense of fair play, it offers nothing to those who want to engage in a genuine search for truth and reality.

All the same thing?

'Buddhism, Islam, Christianity, it's all the same thing anyway!' So declared the sheet of paper. Then I spotted my name, and realised that this was the subject I had to address at Cambridge University.

Trinity Great Hall was packed. Buddhists, Sikhs, Muslims, Christians – mingled with those of no faith at all. I felt that in honesty I had to address the issue in the most straightforward manner possible.

"Christianity is not the same as other faiths. Its claims are superior. For it offers not a religion which tells us about God and ourselves. It brings us into a personal relationship with God himself. The founders of Islam and Buddhism both lie in the grave. Christianity maintains that Jesus is alive, bringing the life of God directly into people today. Dismiss it, reject it, or disprove it – but never place it on the same basis as other faiths. For if true, it outdistances them all. Until you have disposed of it, other faiths will always be inferior to it, for you must judge a faith on the basis of the claims it makes.'

This may not sound like the way to win friends and influence people. Yet it is the traditional assertion of the Christian faith. Why should Christians not proclaim it boldly? In conversation with representatives of Islam I have not encountered any resistance to Christians expressing their own convictions. Rather they are surprised at the suggestion of some Christian ministers that Christianity and Islam should ever be regarded as equally correct. They agree that their conflicting claims deserve examination, not indifference.

The same argument equally applies to other faiths, for all are radically different to one another.

The difference between world faiths

Islam, Judaism and Christianity maintain that there is one God, Hinduism points to a multiplicity of gods while Buddhists search for reality within themselves.

Jewish thought is devoid of any concept of original sin. Buddhism denies the possibility of sin against a supreme being. Muslims have an idea of sin, so concentrate on following a carefully prescribed moral code. Hinduism has no concept of sin. Christianity recognises the existence of Satan, the presence of sin, and the possibility of divine forgiveness.

Hinduism sees life as determined by fate. Zionists look to an external relationship with God based on national identity. Islam views all good and evil as coming from the will of Allah. Buddhism denies the existence of a personal God. Christianity maintains that he arrived in a manger in Bethlehem.

Before one even begins to explore the multitude of other differences, one conclusion is inevitable – these faiths are not the same. They are mutually contradictory.

Today it has become common to assume the validity of many pathways to God, to deny the existence of absolute truth, and to extol the significance of multi-faith worship. This may sound a comfortable theory, but it bears little resemblance to reality. It reduces truth to the level of individual belief determined by personal experience. Any notion of absolute truth is rejected – it would simply not exist.

This convenient argument offers a solution to the problem of competing faiths. It certainly appeals to a secular mind-set that seeks to avoid religious convictions. *What it fails to recognise is that its perceived impartiality is not equally acceptable to those of all faiths.*

Prince Charles might well declare his desire one day to act as 'Defender of faith' rather than of 'the faith'. This would make him Defender of all faiths. Without being uncharitable, we have to question whether other faiths would actually want him to act in this capacity? While the denial that any one faith is true for all might appear fair to the adherents of every religion – that is simply not the case. Followers of the Baha'i faith would plead for mutual forbearance and acceptance between religions. Hindus believe that all faiths should be tolerated because each is seen as pointing in the same direction. However, many Muslims, Jews and Christians disagree with this analysis, believing in the exclusive claims associated with their particular faith.

This sometimes comes as a surprise to those who would believe that only extremists choose to highlight the differences between those of different faiths. In fact sincere believers in both Islam and Christianity will honestly concede the major differences between them.

A leading expert on mission has put it this way:

> Truth is not a matter of pride or humility. It is a matter of fact. Islam says Jesus wasn't crucified. We say he was. Only one of us can be right. Judaism says Jesus was not the Messiah. We say he was. Only one of us can be right. Hinduism says that God has *often* been incarnate. We say only once. And we can't both be right... Any intelligent person could decide that all religions are wrong. Any intelligent person could decide that one is right and the rest wrong. But no intelligent person can seriously believe that all religions are essentially the same. (Dr Peter Cotterell in *London Bible College Review*, [Summer 1989]).

Instead of presenting all faiths as equal or identical, clear thinking lies in an honest examination and assessment of their differences. This should not result in hostility but a courteous articulation of the issues in an honest spirit of enquiry and debate.

Disagreement is not the same as persecution, and the former should never be allowed to lead to the latter. We all need to learn how to disagree, without being disagreeable about it. Intolerance and bigotry can never be consistent with the Christian gospel. Neither should we accept a weak-willed abdication of our responsibility to declare Christian truth to all who will listen. Instead we need to be prepared both to talk and to listen, maintaining individual freedoms while resisting the temptation to compromise the Christian message.

Only one way?

Recently my wife Ruth attended an Open Evening for one of our children. She spoke to the Religious Studies teacher who queried how our son would cope with learning about Islam that year.

Frankly, Ruth could see no problem. To discover the details of another faith scarcely constituted a difficulty. The teacher was surprised, but then commented, 'Well, of course, it doesn't really matter what religion one follows. Islam, Buddhism, Christianity, each is truth for its own adherents. For those of no faith, well that is truth for them too. We can each leave one another to our own beliefs.'

The claims of Jesus are exclusive   Ruth had to express her objection, for Christianity does not allow such a comfortable option. The claims of Jesus were exclusive, he left us no opportunity to bracket him with others. As Paul reminded Timothy, 'there is one mediator between God and men, the man Christ Jesus' (1 Tim 2:5).

The traditional Christian view is to echo the words of Jesus when he announced that he was the only way to know God as Father (Jn 14:6). Salvation depends on an overt knowledge of Jesus Christ, for he alone is the revelation of God's love to humankind. Saving faith comes through his sacrificial death on the cross and resurrection. The Bible alone provides the written record of God's truth. Millions have never heard of Jesus, and unless Christian mission is furthered as a matter of urgency, myriads more will face a lost eternity.

Historically this has come to be known as the *exclusivist* approach. This represents the standard approach of Christianity to other faiths. In the Old Testament, idolatrous practices and indigenous Canaanite religious beliefs were unequivocally denounced (Ex 20:1-5; Deut 5:6-7; 7:1-6; 13:1–14:2; Josh 24:14-25; Is 41:5-7; Jer 10:1-16). The apostles asserted that salvation was only possible through Jesus Christ (Acts 4:12).

Strongly contrasted to this view is the *inclusivist* position. This

The inclusive view: an alternative?   views Christianity as completing other faiths, because Jesus is hidden within them.

The Roman Catholic theologian, Karl Rahner, has argued that it is possible to be an 'anonymous Christian' and receive salvation through Jesus Christ without contact with either the gospel or the church. He argues that God permeates everything, and can be recognised by the eyes of faith.

His idea is that people are judged, not by the doctrines they agree to, but by the way they actually live. This point may be attractive and important, yet in reacting against faith that is intellectual only, and not lived out, Rahner takes his point too far. The end result is a good looking house, but minus its foundations.

Similarly Hans Küng has suggested that we need to search for echoes and reflections of the Spirit of Jesus in other faiths. He prescribes two forms of salvation. The ordinary way is open to the majority who have never been meaningfully exposed to Christianity, and the extraordinary way is reserved for the comparative few who have encountered Christ.

What these ideas ignore is the fact that other religions – even if they accept the idea of salvation – reject the notion that Jesus Christ is their means for receiving it! They see this offer of Christian citizenship as unasked for, and unwanted.

A modification of this view is the *pluralist* position advocated by the philosopher, John Hick, among many others. He has criticised Christianity for placing itself at *The pluralist position* the centre of a spiritual solar system, making other faiths revolve around it as the 'sun'. He argues that God is the centre and Christianity should simply join other faiths as 'planets' revolving around him. The suggestion is that God is the same in every faith, even those that believe in many gods. As for Jesus, his identity only rested in what people recognised him as being, not in his own nature.

By this reasoning all religions ultimately lead to the one God. He inspires all their scriptures. God is seen as being in all things and can therefore be encountered without Jesus being involved.

These three positions can be outlined in this form:-

PLURALIST	EXCLUSIVIST	INCLUSIVIST
Equality of all religions.	Respect for other religions and their followers but not acceptance of their beliefs.	Positive view of other religions.
Jesus one religious leader pointing to the same truth as others.	God was revealed in Jesus, Jesus brings us to know his Father.	God's Spirit is present in all creation – part of God is revealed in all things.
Universalist – all can be saved.	Only believers inherit eternal life.	All faiths offer hope of eternal life from Jesus.
Every person possesses innate religious awareness.	God's saving power is only in Jesus.	God can bring salvation to others apart from an encounter with Jesus.
All religions are equally true.	Other religions are in error concerning salvation, Jesus, and other basic doctrines.	Other religions paved the way for Jesus.
Jesus Christ is replaced by other figures in different faiths.	Jesus Christ is the only way to God.	Jesus Christ is hidden in other faiths.
Christianity is one religious option among many.	Christianity stands apart from other religions – others must be judged by it.	Christianity completes all other religions.
All scriptures reflect the truth of Absolute Reality.	Christian Scriptures alone are truth.	Other scriptures point to the same truths.
Salvation is available through every faith, no conversion is necessary.	Those in other faiths need conversion.	Greater understanding is required of salvation through other faiths.
Salvation comes through works.	Salvation comes from repentance and faith.	Salvation comes from sincere faith within a religious framework.

The exclusivist perspective faces one major objection – how can people be expected to respond to Jesus if they have never heard of him?

A growing number who hold to the exclusivist position would insist that while Christ is not encountered in non-Christian religions, he can still found by those who are within them. An individual can therefore be saved either inside or outside a religion, but one cannot be saved *by* a religion.

Paul says, in his letter to the Romans, that it is possible for individuals to discern God's eternal power and deity through creation and the prompting of their consciences (Rom 2:14-16).

Recognising that salvation only comes through Jesus Christ and his death for human sin (1 Jn 2:2; 1 Cor 15:3-4), as God's divine *logos* he can still illuminate the heart and mind of an individual sufficiently for them to respond to God's revelation in creation and conscience (Jn 1:9).

God has revealed himself adequately enough for people to abandon human religious effort and place their trust in him. This will only apply to those who have not heard the direct message. Our task is to be Christ's ambassadors. We are called to carry his good news to all those who otherwise might be too blind to see (2 Cor 5:17-20).

The recognition of humanity's need for Jesus was to lead directly to the development of mission, social action and evangelistic initiatives. If Christ is the way to God, then people had to know the truth about Jesus.

The reason this is so important lies in the fact that the Bible reveals the truth that, as human beings, we are enslaved by our own sinful nature (Rom 7:14; Jn 8:34). We endure a condition of slavery to everything that has mastered us in our lives (2 Pet 2:19). As sinners we cannot break through in our own strength, we are condemned to die in our sins (Jn 8:24). After all, we are spiritually dead already (Eph 2:1).

This parlous condition has only one remedy. The punishment of the guilty can only be averted by the death of an innocent man. This requires not just the death of a man, but of a man who is God. As the medieval scholar Anslem said, 'Since no-one save God can make satisfaction for our sins, and no-one save man ought to make it, it is necessary for a God-man to make it' (Anslem, *Why*

God Became Man [Westminster, 1956]). Justice demands satisfaction, and Jesus provided it on a cross (Acts 3:19; Rom 4:25; Gal 1:4; Col 2:13; Heb 7:27).

Jesus boldly announced the slavery of each individual to sin, then declared that the potential for freedom was here and now. That miracle of God's grace could only be accomplished one way: 'So if the Son sets you free, you will be free indeed' (Jn 8:36). This was the truth of God's love. That truth was no mere phenomenon. He was personal, walking and talking with them there.

Jesus claimed to Thomas that he alone was the way, truth and life (Jn 14:6). He used the introductory phrase 'I am' – *ego eimi*, the Greek translation of the name by which God revealed himself to Moses. This phrase shows that it is not what Jesus does, but who he is. No-one will come to know God as Father, he affirms, except 'through me'. So it is not a matter of example, as with a Muslim following Mohammed, but Jesus himself is the way to God.

Consequently, Paul is able to affirm that those who follow other faiths have religion without revelation. They are separate from Christ, foreigners to the covenant of promise, without hope and without God. He indicts them as *atheoi* 'without God'; not without religion, but their religion lacked God (Eph 2:11-13). Humanly-constructed religious creeds do not lead us to God, but away from him.

In Jesus lies the opportunity to receive divine forgiveness. He affirmed that we can arrive at the point of spiritual

The process of conversion

rebirth when we enter God's eternal family. This fact Jesus made clear in his conversation with Nicodemus (Jn 3:3): 'No-one can see the kingdom of God unless he is born again.' Nicodemus was a devout Jew, yet Jesus explained that he needed to experience the truth. It was not enough to just know about it. This truth solely comes through believing in the One his Father sent into the world (v 16). The fruit of the truth is eternal life.

Not everyone will be able to put a date and time on the precise moment of their conversion. For some it will be instantaneous, for others it is a more gradual process. For everyone it is an encounter with the One who is truth itself. Not only does he come to warm our hearts by entering our lives, but he comes to redirect our minds to accept who he is and what as God he requires from us.

This opportunity to receive new life does have restrictions placed upon it. It requires the surrender and obedience of repentant hearts and lives. It insists on the necessity of change in our lifestyles. It demands that we think again as to our priorities and understanding of life. Jesus Christ is never prepared to be a mere appendage, an added-on extra to an old lifestyle, he comes instead to make 'all things new' (Rev 21:5 AV). The offer of God's love arrived in Jesus Christ, but so did the demand to live by his truth. The call was to repent, and to believe (Mk 6:12; Acts 3:19; Rev 2:5).

Conversion comes from surrender to the One who justifies us through faith in him. Justification, or restoration and forgiveness, can only come from One entitled to give it. Faith can only be effective if the One in whom we believe is authentic. If Jesus is less than the way, the truth and the life, then our situation is no more than false. This is the glory of the message... and it is one that we are under divine command to share with others (Mt 28:19-20).

Out of bounds

Other faiths possess different attitudes towards sharing their message. In Islam there is a basic requirement for *da'wah*, inviting others to respond to the message brought by the prophet Mohammed. Generally Islam is a community faith. It is the smallest group within Islam, the Ahmaddiya, who are most likely to try to convert others. A missionary impulse appears in some more recent religious movements like the Baha'i. The Buddha invited his followers to spread his teachings. Neither the Jewish, Jain or Sikh faiths seek to recruit converts. Christianity, in contrast, has always been a missionary faith with a specific mandate for active evangelism.

These different approaches and attitudes can easily create tensions. A recent letter I received from the British *Mission will* Board of Jewish Deputies recorded their deep sense *result in* of unease: *tensions*

The one message that we would like to give to British evangelical Christians is to respect the integrity of religions. Jews, and especially younger Jews, are very upset, appalled and concerned by the growing evangelical movements within the broad Christian church. This is offensive. It is odious.

Aggressive evangelical work amongst Jews, Moslems, Hindus and others, undermines and damages years of dialogue that has been built up, based on good faith between Jews, Christians and members of other groups.'

While wholeheartedly sympathising with the concern, understanding has to be a two-way process. Christians need to be courteous in presenting the truth as we perceive it, equally, those of other faiths must understand that we are duty-bound to do so.

How strongly should we evangelise? We should want to dialogue with those of other faiths and be prepared to understand their perspectives. This does not mean that we relinquish our concern that all people might meet Jesus. The Rev Dr Walter Riggans, General Director of CMJ, has pertinently observed, 'We are often told that, in their relationships with people of other faiths, Christians have to choose between dialogue and evangelism. But we… believe that we should be committed to both. We need to be listeners as well as talkers.'

In some Christian circles intolerance of intolerance has become almost obsessive. When the Archbishop of Canterbury, Dr George Carey, inaugurated the Decade of Evangelism, he brought in Bishop Michael Marshall and Canon Michael Green to encourage and lead the project.

The potential emphasis on direct evangelism and conversion troubled many people. The idea that the special unit with the two Michaels was to be called 'Spearhead', found itself swiftly changed to a more innocuous title, 'Springboard'.

Arguments raged as to whether or not it could be appropriate to target those of other faiths with the Christian message. Missionary agencies like 'Jews for Jesus' found themselves excluded from at least one university campus, on the grounds that their activities were inappropriate within a multi-faith student body!

Faced with the decision about accepting the traditional role of Patron of the Churches Ministry among the Jews, the Archbishop found himself in an impossible situation. Either he antagonised those working for Judaeo-Christian dialogue and co-operation, or he ran the risk of alienating himself from the mission-minded evangelical community.

He declined the Patronage, and I found myself having to declare that, 'The Church of England would not exist if Jewish Christians had denied the message of Jesus to the Jewish people, and then to the rest of the known world.'

I appreciate the awful dilemma faced by the Archbishop. He, and all in strategic positions of authority, need our prayers that they may act with wisdom and integrity. I want to be warmly supportive of Dr Carey, a man for whose integrity and genuine passion for the gospel I have the deepest respect. On this occasion I remain convinced that he was wrong – but few of us are on the firing line over this kind of issue. At least, not yet!

As a contribution to the International Year of Inter Religious Understanding and Cooperation in 1993, the Inter Faith Network in the United Kingdom produced a set of guidelines for Inter Religious *How far should respect and toleration go?* Encounter. This helpful document urged the need for mutual respect and understanding between those of different faiths. It urged sensitivity and courtesy and the avoidance of misrepresentation in our dealings with one another.

This is all good and right. The report concludes that:-

> Living and working together is not always easy. Religion harnesses deep emotions which can sometimes take destructive forms. Where this has happened, we must work hard to bring about reconciliation and understanding. But the truest fruits of religion are healing and positive. We have a great deal to gain from one another. Together, listening and responding with openness and respect, we can move forward to work in ways that acknowledge genuine differences but build on shared hopes and values. (Inter Faith Network, *Living with People of Different Faiths and Beliefs.*)

One can only heartily agree with these sentiments. However, closer analysis reveals that they only represent one half of the story! Protection is urged for those who are challenged by people of other faiths. Barriers are erected against inappropriate proselytisation. No similar protection is offered for those who choose to convert to another faith.

Family hostility and permanent estrangement from the community can often result when a Muslim, Hindu, Sikh or Jewish person decides to become a Christian. There is no attempt to safeguard their right to do this, or to urge tolerance for their decision!

Similarly, no mention is made of the overt persecution meted out to Christians in other lands. Yes, we do need to model tolerance to the Islamic community, but we must insist on the right to religious freedom in Muslim lands for Christians and for Christian converts. To fail in this respect gives the impression that we are apathetic at the fate of our brothers and sisters who endure oppression, and even martyrdom, in other parts of the world.

One other disturbing trend emerges from this report by the Inter Faith Network. It comments that after the Decade of Evangelism was launched, 'Other British faith communities expressed fears that their members might be singled out as targets for conversion… In response, reassurances were given by church leaders that the primary goals of the Decade are the rekindling of the faith of nominal Christians and the drawing in of those with no existing religious commitment.'

In other words, evangelistic initiatives aimed at the conversion of those of other faiths are regarded as entirely inappropriate. If our missionary forbears of the nineteenth century had been aware of this, then half of the current Christian church worldwide would still be unconverted.

Conversion is at the heart of the Christian gospel   The principle of conversion lies at the heart of the Christian gospel. The church has always maintained the right to reach out to others with the good news that arrived in Jesus Christ.

Jesus came to offer freedom. He told those who would hold to his teaching and follow him that their lives would be transformed. For they would then, 'Know the truth, and the truth will set you free ' (Jn 8:32).

What was this truth he had come to reveal? It was that ordinary people of all faiths could be restored to relationship with their Creator. Jesus had arrived to introduce men and women to his Father, and through his death to break down the dividing wall of sin forever (Eph 2:14).

This great liberating truth is discovered at conversion, the moment when as individuals we become reconciled to God. Throughout the centuries people have experienced the guilt, pain and enormous relief of coming to the one who is Truth and encountering his divine forgiveness.

Here is one individual, but very significant example. Born into a wealthy Sikh family in the Punjab he was educated at mission school. Swiftly he grew to hate Christianity *An example: a Sikh convert* and its Bible which was so foreign to him. He publicly burned a copy and led a gang of youths in throwing mud and stones at a local Christian preacher.

At fifteen years of age he contemplated suicide. Searching desperately for any form of spiritual reality he later recalled, 'Praying and waiting and expecting to see Krishna or Buddha, or some other Avatar of the Hindu religion; they appeared not, but a light was shining in the room.' Three days after burning a Bible he had to announce to a thunderstruck father, 'I have seen Jesus Christ! He appeared to me in my room just now. I have become a Christian.'

He boldly cut off his Kev, his bunched hair, knowing that a Sikh shorn of his hair was a Sikh no longer. Estranged from his family, he gave his life to the service of Jesus Christ. His conversion was so complete that he proclaimed the Christian gospel throughout India, and then took the same message to Tibet. From there he never returned. That man was the famous Indian evangelist, Sadhu Sundar Singh.

The Christian commitment to conversion extends as far back as the Damascus road and the dramatic transformation in the life of Saul of Tarsus. While retaining the culture and training of Judaism he unflinchingly preached the need for Jewish people to meet Jesus.

Paul knew his own story of how God had encountered him, and he was unafraid to use it to Jews and Romans alike (Acts 22:1-21; 26:4-18). On Mars Hill, in Athens, Paul acknowledged other beliefs, but refused to recognise their validity. He never arranged an inter-faith service, but announced that the One they unconsciously worshipped as the Unknown God was the Creator of the universe (Acts 17:23-24).

Paul never suggested a gentlemanly dialogue between Zeus and Yahweh in order to establish spiritual authority over the Greeks. He simply announced the good news about Jesus and left them to make their response.

Christians must always recognise sincere convictions at variance with our own, but we do not need to agree that other gods exist. People can be misguided, mistaken or just sincerely wrong.

Conversion lies at the heart of our faith. To forbid us the right to seek to lead others to Jesus is to make us ignore his command and deny our own sincerely held beliefs. Previous generations of Christians have given their lives to protect this freedom. To share the opportunity for every person of every faith to meet Jesus and enjoy the fruits of rebirth is our privilege, and our duty.

8

In the Footsteps of Heroes

We walk in the footsteps of heroes as we take the message of the gospel to other peoples. This chapter considers what lessons we can learn from past heroes of faith and what opposition we should expect.

In the Footsteps of Heroes

I have got no further than this: Every man has a right to utter what he thinks truth, and every other man has a right to knock him down for it. Martyrdom is the test.

Samuel Johnson.

A few days later we were lodged in the prison, and I was terrified as I had never before been in such a dark hole. What a difficult time it was ! With the crowd the heat was stifling; then there was the extortion of the soldiers; and to crown it all, I was tortured with worry for my baby there.

One day... a huge crowd gathered. We walked up to the prisoners' dock. All the others, when questioned, admitted their guilt. Then, when it came to my turn, my father appeared with my son, dragged me from the step, and said: 'Perform the sacrifice – have pity on your baby!'

Hilarianus the governor, who had received his judicial powers as the successor of the late proconsul Minucius Timinianus, said to me: 'Have pity on your father's grey head; have pity on your infant son. Offer the sacrifice for the welfare of the emperors.'

'I will not,' I retorted.

'Are you a Christian?' said Hilarianus.

And I said: 'Yes, I am.'

Then Hilarianus passed sentence on all of us: we were condemned to the beasts, and we returned to prison in high spirits.

But my baby had got used to being nursed at the breast and to staying with me in prison. So I sent the deacon Pomonius straightaway to my father to ask for the baby. But father refused to give him over. But as God willed, the baby had no further desire for the breast, nor did I suffer any inflammation; and so I was relieved of any anxiety for my child and of any discomfort in my breasts (Quoted in *The History of Christianity* [Lion: Tring, 1977]).

The year was 202, the place was Carthage in Africa. The writer was Vibia Perpetua, an upper-class lady who was thrown into prison, along with several slaves, because of her Christian faith. Her martyrdom is reported to have resulted in the conversion of the prison governor.

The early church possessed no technology, few of their leaders lived a long life, they had no buildings, they were denounced as a perverted and impoverished sect – yet within three centuries of the death of her founder the church was the official religion of the Roman Empire.

Why this explosion of faith? The reason for this explosion of faith did not lie in a methodology, in complex structures, or a refined bureaucracy – it can only be attributed to the simple witness of ordinary Christians who just could not keep their faith to themselves. They had found the truth, and were prepared to suffer and even die for it.

We may look for programmes, projects or methods by which to advance the Christian message. The early church possessed a different strategy. Those Christians recognised that Jesus had brought the truth of God into the world. They knew that this message needed to be carried to the far corners of the globe. Having received the power of the Holy Spirit their task was simply to go and share the good news. This they did, and the results were astounding.

IN THE FOOTSTEPS OF HEROES 141

The word *marturia,* from which we draw 'martyr', means testimony, and its verb denotes bearing witness. It embraces not only the idea of verbal communication, but also the idea of giving living testimony to the truth. In true Christian witness, word and example must be united to give a powerful expression of the truth. John the Baptist came to bear witness to the light (Jn 1:7; 3:26) and to announce him as Son of God (Jn 1:34). This is precisely the task that faces us today. We have a message to share and a life to live which will demonstrate the truth of what we have to say.

Our task: to witness

A dictionary definition puts it in this way: '*Witness* – knowledge brought in proof; testimony of a fact; that which furnishes proof; one who sees or has personal knowledge of a thing; one who gives evidence... *bear witness* – to give, or be, evidence' (Chambers English Dictionary [W. & R. Chambers: Cambridge, 1988]).

Jesus deliberately called his followers to act as his witnesses (Acts 1:8). Their testimony was not to be confined to their public proclamations, but would include every aspect of their conversation and conduct. As they bore witness to the truth their message would be contagious, it would spread like wildfire – simply because it was true.

It is astonishing to register the growth and development of Christianity from a Palestinian backwater, to the heart of the Lateran Palace of the emperors of Rome. As one leading missiologist has acutely observed,

> Perhaps the most spectacular triumph of Christianity in history is its conquest of the Roman Empire in roughly twenty decades. We know very little about this period. Our lack of knowledge makes much of it a mystery, and what happened to Christianity sounds impossible, almost unbelievable (Ralph Winter, 'The Ten Epochs of Redemptive History' in *Perspectives on the World Christian Movement* [William Carey Library: Pasadena, 1981]).

The only conceivable answer lies in the unique quality of the early Christians' witness to Jesus. By this means they effectively transformed the world around them (Acts 17:6). The lessons we can learn from their example remain invaluable today, for in seeking to learn from those early disciples we are truly walking in the footsteps of heroes.

A church without walls

A superficial reading of the Acts of the Apostles might suggest that Paul and Barnabas, along with their friends and colleagues, were the only pioneer missionaries among the first generation of Christian believers.

Despite early hesitancy, the other apostles almost certainly travelled far and wide in their desire to share the gospel. Peter preached in Rome, and John maintained a long and successful ministry in the province of Asia.

As to the specific operation of the rest, we are less certain. Tradition is mixed with legend, and it is usually difficult to untangle the two.

While one might be sceptical of stories that Joseph of Arimathea carried the gospel to Britain, there is stronger traditional support for Mark's involvement in the foundation of the church in Alexandria. Thaddeus may well have helped to establish the church in Edessa, and Thomas is traditionally believed to have carried the Christian message to India.

Even when taken alongside Paul's extensive missionary journeys, these initiatives do not begin to explain the fantastic expansion and growth enjoyed by the early Christian church. Even the most agnostic historian is perplexed by the rate at which Christianity spread throughout the Roman world.

The early evangelists were not professionals The plain fact of the matter is that the gospel was not disseminated throughout the Roman world by either preachers or professionals. It was thousands of anonymous believers who simply gossiped the gospel, and discussed their new-found faith with their friends and contemporaries.

These unrecorded evangelists, men and women, were scattered throughout the Roman world as traders, business people, refugees, soldiers and the like.

Christianity was therefore concentrated in predominantly urban areas, and was based on the key Roman cities. It spread along the trade routes normally, though not exclusively, through the planting of churches. These then became missionary communities seeking to evangelise their localities. None of these churches possessed buildings. They simply used their homes.

In the second century AD one of the earliest Christian apologists, Justin Martyr, gave his life in the cause of the gospel. When interrogated in a hostile pagan court the conversation went like this:

> Judge: 'Where do you have your meetings?'
> Justin: 'Wherever we can. Our God fills heaven and earth.'
> Judge: 'Tell me where!'
> Justin: 'I live upstairs in the house of Martin... If anyone wishes to come in to me there, I pass on to him the true doctrine.'
> (Quoted in John Foster, *The First Advance* [SPCK: London, 1972]).

Private homes became evangelistic outposts dedicated to the spreading of Christian truth. These provided the hub for a vast people movement which would carry the gospel worldwide.

The quality of Christian witness was such that most new converts were originally attracted by just a casual contact with Christianity. Often this interest was aroused by witnessing a martyrdom, observing the manner in which Christians cared for strangers, or simply receiving hospitality from the church.

Personal witness was the most common form of evangelism employed by the early church. Friendship became the means of many people being attracted to the truth of Jesus Christ. Casual encounters also proved, time and again, the opportunity for sharing the good news. *Spontaneous personal witness was common*

Outstanding church leaders were often converted through personal acquaintance. Justin Martyr came to faith through a conversation with an old man in Ephesus. Cyprian, later to become Bishop of Carthage, was converted through talking to a church elder. The scholar and philosopher-theologian, Origen, came from a Christian family in Alexandria and the foundation for his knowledge of Christian truth originally came from his parents.

Celsus, a second-century opponent of the Christian faith, indicated the effectiveness of this kind of spontaneous Christian witness. He recorded the way in which uneducated Christians seized every opportunity to witness to those they met. So confident were they of Christian truth that they would confront pagan scholars with their opinions. Whether or not they won the argument was irrelevant to them. They knew that truth would provide its own vindication.

This remains a vital lesson for the church today. Too often we confine our ideas of Christian witness to the activities of gifted professionals, or the opportunities provided by special meetings or missions within our churches. Many Christians remain unaware of the fact that, even today, more people come to faith in Jesus Christ through contact with Christian friends than by attending meetings. Both approaches have their value, but personal witness is often necessary to attract someone to even attend a meeting!

For too long we have concentrated our efforts in the local church on special initiatives, often at the expense of encouraging consistent witnessing lifestyles. Without ignoring those special gifts which God gives to some of his servants, we must never be guilty of rejecting our own potential.

The Great Commission applies to all believers
A groundswell of concern has emerged in recent years that the church must recognise that the commission of Jesus applies to all believers. He instructed his people to wait to receive power from above in order that they might then go out to witness to the truth of all that they had seen and heard.

For as long as the majority of evangelical Christians are content to leave the task of prayer, witness and evangelism to what happens in our religious buildings, we will have failed to grasp that God intends to use each one of us in our everyday situations. For he has called each one of us to be his witnesses, at home, in our communities, throughout our nation, and ultimately to the far corners of the globe (Acts 1:8).

Few are given the specific ministry of the evangelist, with the accompanying spiritual anointing to lead many to the point where they actively embrace the truth of Jesus Christ. But we can all be the agents used to lead others one step forward on their pilgrimage to arrive at faith. Sometimes we may face the challenge of joining a neighbour, colleague, or friend at the specific point of commitment. This will be rare. Often we will simply be the means of taking people one step forward.

I have often found this contemporary adaptation of the Engel Scale to be a helpful illustration of the process in which people engage in their journey to faith.

Steps to Christ

10 | Decision to surrender to Christ

9 | Acceptance of the implications

8 | Acceptance of Christian truth

7 | Understand the implications of this

6 | Grasp the truth about Jesus

5 | Decide to investigate Jesus

4 | Interest in Jesus Christ

3 | Contact with Christians

2 | Some awareness of God

1 | No awareness of God

(Taken from Laurence Singlehurst ed. *The Evangelism Toolkit* [March for Jesus: London, 1991]).

We do not all enjoy preaching skills, musical abilities, or the courage and gifts to share our faith on someone's doorstep or in the open air. Yet we are each called and com- *The quality of* missioned, in direct succession to the apostles, to act *our lives makes* as witnesses to the truth (Mt 28:19-20). This may be *the bigger* through our prayers, conversation or actions. In each *impact* way we can give effective testimony to the reality that we have encountered in Jesus.

It is almost inevitable that the quality of our lives and the genuineness of our character make the biggest human contribution towards people who are not Christians developing an interest in Jesus Christ. We need to live in a way that demands an explanation – witness through words so often follows witness by our lives.

The early church existed without walls. One of the major reasons for its fantastic growth was that for nearly three hundred years they were devoid of specialist buildings. With no need to concentrate on maintenance, their efforts were focused on gaining new adherents. Unable to gather in a ghetto, their Christian life and witness had to be earthed in the community in which they lived.

Buildings have their uses, but need to be employed for the community, not just the congregation. Otherwise they can concentrate our attention on looking in, rather than out, and view the church as a building rather than as people, which the New Testament continually affirms. Over the last two decades twentieth-century obsession with meetings, fabric and structures has begun to be replaced by the conviction that there is far more to genuine Christian living than the performance of religious routines. Many have begun to believe that a maintenance complex is being replaced by a fresh desire to engage in more 'risky living'.

Such people have insisted that the time has come to return to that earlier pioneering spirit where each believer knew that God could use them as witnesses to his truth; so the church knew what it was to grow in a hostile environment where witnesses lived for Jesus in the certainty that, if accused of being Christians, there was more than enough evidence to ensure their conviction.

In such an atmosphere truth becomes a living, breathing reality. By living as its witnesses we deliver truth from being regarded as mere abstract reality divorced from our contemporary situation. Instead we draw the attention of our neighbours and friends to the truth we have encountered; we then prepare the way to tell them his name – Jesus!

Truth worth dying for

Such truth has a price tag attached. Christianity never offers an easy way. Servants of Christ are called to deny themselves and take up their cross in order to follow Jesus (Mt 16:24; Mk 8:34; Lk 9:23).

This was certainly the experience of the early church. *The cost of* For three hundred years the church suffered spasmodic *witnessing* outbreaks of persecution. Accused of cannibalism (for eating and drinking the body and blood of Jesus), incest (for insisting on the need to 'love one another'), and licentious banquets (the love-feast or fellowship meal). Christians were continually harassed and misunderstood by the authorities.

When Christians were persecuted the secular powers found that they could not extinguish the flame; instead it grew brighter! Many pagans were deeply impressed by Christian patience and conviction in the face of extreme suffering. It was the quality of their lives, and the conviction of the message they carried, that transported the Christian gospel throughout the Roman Empire.

The Roman historian Tacitus records that, 'In their deaths they were made a mockery. They were covered in the skins of wild animals, torn to death by dogs, crucified or set on fire, so that when darkness fell they burned like torches in the night. Nero opened up his own gardens for this spectacle and gave a show in the arena.' But still the church grew.

Despite the careful responses of early Christian apologists, their defence of the truth was blithely ignored. Society often needed scapegoats. The second-century Christian writer, Tertullian, recorded the regular tendency to blame the Christians for any natural disaster. He sarcastically commented, 'If the River Tiber reaches the walls, if the River Nile does not rise to the fields, if the sky does not move or the earth does, if there is famine, if there is plague, the cry is at once: 'The Christians to the lion!' What, all of them to one lion?' (Tertullian, *Apology,* tr. T. R. Glover [Loeb Library]).

Major outbreaks of persecution took place in the first century by the Roman emperors Nero and Domitian, and in the third century under Decius and Diocletian. However, the second-century correspondence between Pliny, the Roman governor of Bithynia, and the Emperor Trajan indicates that persecution was the normal treatment to be expected by Christians.

This was unusual in the Roman world. Minority religions were readily tolerated, and their gods were absorbed into the Roman pantheon to be worshipped alongside every other deity. The problem with Christians lay.in their stubborn refusal to accept that anyone possessed the truth apart from themselves.

Christians insisted that there was only one God, and that he could only be encountered through his Son. They refused to worship the Emperor and therefore laid themselves open to the charge of treason. Many refused to even burn a pinch of incense in his honour, because this would be viewed as disloyalty to Jesus Christ.

Those who did compromise in this way were termed 'lapsi', the lapsed, and their re-entry into the church was often a lengthy and onerous process. For the early church truth was not a negotiable issue. Even if one knew that other gods were false and illusory, an unequivocal stand for the true God was demanded.

What made the difference to public opinion was the behaviour of the Christians. Their witness was used by the Holy Spirit to alter the attitudes of their opponents. These would eventually change 'their violent and tyrannical disposition, being overcome either by the constancy which they have witnessed in their neighbours' lives, or by the extraordinary forbearance they have observed in their fellow-travellers when defrauded, or by the honesty of those with whom they transacted business. (Justin Martyr, *Apology* – quoted in ed. J.Stevenson, *A New Eusebius* [SPCK: London, 1957]).

This second-century account of how the Christians lived down slanderous accusations made against them indicates how vital is the contribution of Christian lives which testify to the truth. Tertullian affirmed that the blood of the martyrs became the seed from which the church could grow.

Today we may not find ourselves called upon to die for our faith. We cannot rely on this assumption, for the twentieth century has seen more people martyred for the truth than all the preceding nineteen centuries put together. But even if we continue to enjoy freedom of religion, we will still find it costly to be Christian – for opposition can come in many forms. The notion that Christians will not have to face opposition and persecution, both direct and indirect, is dangerous.

I vividly remember the morning that my wife, Ruth, and I were dramatically woken up at 6 am to hear our door being kicked in.

The burglar who had gained access in this unorthodox fashion proceeded to steal Ruth's handbag containing the money she had received for her birthday, and made his escape before I could arrive downstairs.

That afternoon Ruth rang the Evangelical Alliance offices to inform me that our oldest son, Kris, had been on Clapham Common with a Christian friend, and both lads had been mugged at knife point and robbed of their mountain bikes.

Returning home after a fruitless attempt to help the police recover the bikes, I found Ruth standing in the study with a small bullet hole in the window. She had been shot at with an air rifle.

It is not often that one has a burglary, a mugging, and a shooting in one day! However, it was the launch day for a significant new initiative in which we were engaged. Ruth grinned and said 'Well, we must be doing something right somewhere!'

Jesus promised that his followers would have to endure persecution (Mt 5:11; Jn 15:20). This was the experience of the earliest Christians (1 Thess 3:4; 2 Tim 3:12; Heb 11:37), and it remains our expectation today. If we are not physically mistreated, our allegiance to truth will still render us liable to misunderstanding and verbal abuse.

Sadly the church often seeks to live as if this were not to be expected. We readily seek to accommodate ourselves to the cultural norms of our times. Indeed a calm and gentle breeze appears to drift across the church in Western Europe. Occasional ripples emerge *We adapt too easily to our local culture's norms* to disturb its bland surface. The odd internal disagreement, doctrinal controversy or financial need disrupts the *status quo*, but these swiftly pass away. New organisations emerge, old ones continue, evangelism is just an occasional special effort in the life of the church. We observe little change, small growth, and negligible impact on a population whose comment on Christian credibility has been made with their feet.

We are entitled to ask whether Christians still realise that there is a war on? For too long we have listened to the glib prophets of an easy going *The war is still on!* triumphalism who predict comfort and security for God's people. Expectations of health and prosperity rest uneasily with faith in One who had nowhere to lay his head (Mt 8:20). When faced with a tax bill for himself and Simon Peter, Jesus had to borrow a coin from the mouth of a conveniently floating fish! (Mt 17:27).

We live in exciting times, when the potential for genuine growth and development within church life appears considerable. If this is to happen, it will not be without opposition. Satan will mobilise his forces and society may become more hostile to the truth we proclaim. We need to prepare for this. Truth has always been an expensive commodity and we dare not compromise its message and authority in order to win approval from our neighbours, colleagues and friends.

The warning of Scripture is explicit. One day every knee will bow at the name of Jesus, and the truth of who he is will be on the lips of everyone (Phil 2:10). For millions of people that moment will be too late and the certainty of a Godless eternity will beckon them.

If we really believe this to be true, then an enormous task lies ahead of us. We are faced with the challenge of presenting truth to those who have ignored or rejected it. We cannot allow ourselves the luxury of escapism, for if we do believe in hell, then there can be no excuse for failing to announce the truth to those who have remained indifferent to it. This is our task – whatever the consequences may be!

As an old and trusted friend, Ian Coffey, has often commented, 'Most evangelicals today live as covert universalists. They must believe that in the end everyone will be saved. This constitutes the only charitable reason for our appalling failure to share the truth with others.'

Most Christians reject with their mind the notion of universalism, the idea that everyone will get to heaven regardless of what they believe, but many find the prospect of anyone going to hell difficult to accept. We can easily say we believe in hell and yet hope it is not true! Whatever our understanding of the exact nature of future judgement and punishment (and Christians have many different views!) this should motivate us to action, not lead us into paralysis. For conversion is the only appropriate response to the love Jesus has shown to us on the cross, and the only means by which the Holy Spirit can enable us to live for God and others here, and then enjoy the privileges of eternity with Jesus.

Ridicule and rejection may well follow a more aggressive and straightforward presentation of the truth. The early church believed their message to be worth dying for. We have no reason to differ.

To the far corners...

By the year AD 150 flourishing churches existed in nearly all the Roman provinces from Syria to Rome. To the west there were churches in such far-flung outposts as Gaul (modern France), and Christianity had already arrived in Britain. There were, to the east, churches beyond the eastern fringes of the Roman empire. Strong churches could be found in the major cities, and probably the churches of Alexandria and Carthage were already in existence by this time.

The spread of the gospel was greatly facilitated by the ease of travel and common language which existed in the Roman world. The *Pax Romana* ensured a relatively peaceful co-existence throughout the Empire. Meanwhile the spiritual emptiness of the various 'mystery religions' created a hunger for truth in the hearts of men and women. As Christians travelled in the course of business and other responsibilities, so the message of Jesus went with them.

Church growth was often immediate, widespread, and sustained. Referring to the Roman world, Justin Martyr, the Christian apologist, maintained that the gospel had spread among all classes of people.

> There is not a single race of men, whether barbarians or Greeks, or whatever they may be called, nomads or vagrants, or herdsmen dwelling in tents, among whom prayers and giving of thanks are not offered through the name of the crucified Jesus. (Justin Martyr, *Dialogue with Trypho*.)

Progressively Christians became even more aware of their responsibility towards the wider world. Missionaries journeyed to remote parts, often at grave personal risk to their lives.

In Armenia a pioneer missionary named Gregory was ordered to lay garlands on the altar of the goddess Anahit. When he refused, he was imprisoned and tortured. The quality of his endurance under persecution persuaded the king of Armenia to turn to Christ, and they worked together to make the kingdom Christian.

Origen foresaw the possibility that one day the whole world could be evangelised. He encouraged the church to pursue this task, and noted that 'Many people, not only barbarians, but even in the Empire, have not yet heard the word of Christ'. He urged that 'The gospel has not yet been preached to all nations, since it has not reached the Chinese or the Ethiopians beyond the river, and only small parts of the more remote and barbarous tribes.'

By AD 250 a significant Christian minority could be found in several countries to the east of the Roman Empire. Within a further fifty years the strong Christian groups which existed in almost every province of the Roman Empire had become a majority in parts of Africa and Asia Minor.

Finally, in AD 312, the Emperor Constantine himself gave his official support to the Christian faith.

Stories of personal heroism and devotion litter the pages of Christian history as the church endeavoured to take the truth throughout the Roman world, and beyond. Two young men, Aidesius and Frumentius, were shipwrecked on the Red Sea and taken into slavery at the Ethiopian court. Despite encountering considerable opposition from the king, they gained his eventual favour, were awarded high office at court, and won a number of converts. From their efforts came the birth of the Ethiopian church around AD 330, and a few years later Frumentius was consecrated as its first bishop.

Such people refused to be blinded by the comforts or discouragements of the wider world. They had discovered the truth, and found that they could not keep it to themselves.

They were aware that their message was the truth for all peoples. So the early church sought to make it as culturally relevant as possible. One authority on missions confirms the impression thus:

> The missionary church of the first three centuries used the methods and adopted the media that it felt to be consistent with its calling. Its members walked the roads, appealed for

legitimate protection, won converts from God-fearers, and translated its message into the cultural thought-forms of Greek-speaking society. (Maurice Sinclair, *Ripening Harvest, Gathering Storm,* [MARC: London, 1988]).

Such a commitment can never be devoid of personal sacrifice. The warlike Goths scarcely seemed like prime candidates for evangelisation. One individual, Ulfilas, became the key instrument used by God to establish a church among these people. Half-Goth himself, he laboured for forty years (AD 343-383) as a missionary-evangelist among the Goths. He carefully trained and nurtured his converts, and translated most of the Bible into their language.

The result was the preservation of the church and the continuation of its northern advance at a time when the Roman Empire was starting to collapse. The personal price for Ulfilas was measured by hardship, pain, and continual danger to his life.

It did not take much of a leap to carry that sort of commitment from their own geographical territory to neighbouring countries and beyond. John Chrysostom, the Patriarch of Constantinople, affirmed that '"Go and make disciples of all nations" was not said for the apostles only, but for us also'. This truth was recovered by the pioneers of the great missionary explosion of the nineteenth century, and remains equally true for us today. As twentieth-century theologian, Emil Brunner, pithily confirmed, 'The church exists by mission as a fire exists by burning.'

Unfortunately, the twentieth-century church has often been reluctant to acknowledge this principle. While the nineteenth century witnessed massive missionary expansion, today major opinion-forming influences in our society militate against a mission mind-set.

Politically, we remember the abuses of colonialism with a bitter taste in our mouths. Alongside a recognition that we no longer wish to export our sense *Barriers to mission today* of civilisation has come a resistance to taking our faith to other cultures. Secular opinion has focused on the need to tolerate those of other faiths, not to convert them!

As pluralistic thinking has permeated the church, so has come an antipathy towards the attempt to convert anyone from one faith to another. It is enough for someone to believe something! After all, if every religion is equal, and truth simply a matter of personal choice, there is no need to proclaim the gospel. It has been cynically observed that if there is a God he will save everyone anyway.

Much of the glamour of mission has subsided. Bible-smuggling to the Communist bloc is now superseded by training programmes and translation work. Destinations like Africa and China have often been replaced by the less dramatic needs of Belgium or Italy.

'Aid' cannot replace mission Churches have tended to become happier with seeing 'mission' in terms of physical aid, education and social projects. While this has been a significant contribution to our understanding of the comprehensive character of the gospel, it can unintentionally reduce the commitment to direct proclamation and church planting.

Truth needs to be told. The model of the early church is a vivid reminder of that imperative upon our lives. God's intention was always that his truth should reach all nations (Rom 9:23-26; 1 Pet 2:9-10; Hos 1:10; Rom 11:23). Jesus commissioned his followers to go out in his name (Lk 9:1-6, 10:17), and challenged them to go and make disciples out of every nation (Mt 28:19-20), a command which remains equally valid today.

Mission is therefore a two-dimensional strategy. Jesus instructed his disciples to begin in Jerusalem, but then to expand their horizons (Acts 1:8). What begins as personal witness and evangelism in our own locality can swiftly become a concern for mission worldwide.

The fulfilling of the Great Commission must represent our supreme purpose. Telling others incorporates both evangelism and mission. Our local activities in Christian witness will contribute to the global task of mission. The local church should always recognise that it is part of the world church and adopt a strategy which reflects this fact.

Local churches should organise evangelism While spontaneous evangelism, taking opportunities as they arise, is generally an individual activity – organised evangelism is primarily the responsibility of the local church. Every healthy church requires evangelistic goals and a long-term strategy to achieve these. These necessitate immediate plans, alongside actual activities in order to fulfil the strategy.

This process can simply be summarised.

PURPOSE –   The Great Commission provides our timeless objective.

GOALS –   Long-term, achievable and general aims.

STRATEGY –   Targeted means to achieve our goals.

PLANS –   Specific, detailed, timetabled short-term schemes.

ACTIVITIES –   Present opportunities, both one-off and ongoing.

A missionary orientated church should be committed to active engagement in local evangelism. An evangelistic church needs to be actively supporting mission beyond its own locality. In this way we will continue to fulfil the work of Jesus in his Great Commission: '…go and make disciples of all nations, baptising them in the name of the Father and of the Son and of the Holy Spirit, and teaching them to obey everything I have commanded you. And surely I am with you always, to the very end of the age' (Mt 28: 19-20).

In order to fulfil this objective and be obedient to the truth, a fresh emphasis on mission is essential in the life of the local church. As individuals we all have a role to play in enlarging our vision beyond the U.K. in order to pray, support and participate in mission within a context outside of our own.

Indigenous church growth will be our aim in every country – but each needs the love and support of brothers and sisters elsewhere. If truth is to spread worldwide, then we all have a part to play. But we do not act alone!

The Holy Spirit is God the Father's gift to our evangelistic enterprise! Without him we could do nothing, for he provides the fire in our hearts. There is an inseparable link between the Holy Spirit and the *The Holy Spirit provides the fire* fulfilment of God's purposes in using his people to proclaim the good news. It is the Holy Spirit who is our mentor as he guides us in proclaiming the truth about Jesus (Jn 14:17, 26; 15:26; 16:13).

Unless the Holy Spirit is active, then all our efforts are

worthless (Jn 16:8ff). He is the one who leads us into all truth, who was the motivating power behind the heroes of faith, and who is with us and in us today (Mt 28:20).

In John 20, when Jesus breathed on his disciples in order that they might receive the Holy Spirit, he sent them to the world in the same way that the Father had sent Jesus.

In other words, they were to go as suffering servants, humble and obedient. For that reason they would need the Holy Spirit, for he is always given in order that the objective of mission might be accomplished (Jn 20:21-22).

We therefore pray that we might be filled with the Holy Spirit as we go to proclaim the truth about Jesus. This is vital, because he alone can bring conviction of sin, fear of God and illumination of truth to the hearts and lives of unbelievers.

Zechariah 8:18-23 makes it very clear that there is a link between prayer and irresistible evangelism. People who seek God are transformed so that unbelievers can see the truth of Christ in them.

Equipped in this way we too can follow in the footsteps of heroes of the truth. It once took ordinary men and women to turn their world upside down; the same remains true today.

We may not encounter the same obstacles as our predecessors. For them evangelism was 'a very daunting prospect... involving social odium, political danger, the charge of treachery to the gods and the state, the insinuation of horrible crimes and calculated opposition from a combination of sources more powerful than at any time since' (Michael Green, *Evangelism through the Local Church* [Hodder and Stoughton: London, 1990]).

The opposition we face may be more subtle. The fact remains that our world is still hostile to the truth. This does not excuse us, for we have no right to be selfish with the truth – we have a divine mandate to share it!

We walk in the footsteps of heroes, witnessing, suffering and taking truth beyond ourselves in order that the message of Jesus might permeate to the ends of the earth – for then the King will return!

9
Conduct Unbecoming

We have to witness to the truth in our lives as well as our words: we have to 'walk where we talk'. In this chapter we look at the need for complete honesty and openness with one another and with God if we are to be credible as Christians.

Conduct Unbecoming

Of right and wrong he taught
Truths as refin'd as ever Athens heard;
And (strange to tell!) he practis'd what he preached
John Armstrong.

It had not been a good month. The news of five failed marriages among church leaders and personal friends was unparalleled in my experience. Then the phone rang with a simple shattering message.

'Our minister has just had to resign. I'm trying to help sort out some of the confused pieces in a very messy jigsaw. He's been sleeping with one of the congregation, and this appears to be the third affair he's had in over ten years of ministry here. His wife did not suspect a thing – and nor did anyone in the church.'

One can only imagine the sense of betrayal felt by both his family and the church he had faithfully pastored. People knew and trusted him. Now the longstanding deceit and adultery were exposed, with dreadful consequences for all involved.

Only a few years ago this type of incident would be almost unheard of. Now it occurs often enough for surprise and disappointment to have replaced horror and incredulity. We live

159

in a society that has peddled its own moral values long enough for the church to have become infected along with everyone else.

Nor is moral failing among Christians confined to the sphere of sexual sins. I well remember visiting a respected Christian leader in prison – his crime was one of embezzlement over a lengthy period of time.

These instances are not examples of reprehensible 'one-off' lapses, but of continued rebellion against God's revealed will for our lives. In each case the individual conscience is corrupted by giving into temptation with the tragic conclusion that, 'They claim to know God, but by their actions they deny him' (Titus 1:16). The result is a 'seared conscience' and rejection of God's desires for us.

Andrew was a highly-respected member of his church in a small town in Hampshire. He was a local solicitor, preached regularly in the church, played an active role in church leadership, and was generally liked and trusted by people both inside and outside the congregation. But all the time, Andrew was leading a double life. As a solicitor, many people trusted him to invest or move large amounts of money for them. Over the course of three years, Andrew siphoned off this money into a number of personal bank accounts. He then used it to buy a large house, several cars and a number of exotic holidays.

When police finally caught up with him, his double life was exposed. The shock waves were severe: a colleague committed suicide; one of Andrew's clients lost all his life savings and died because of stress; Andrew's wife divorced him; the church was devastated.

In 1993, Andrew was sentenced to five years in prison. (Taken from C. Calver, S. Chilcraft, P. Meadows, S. Jenkins, *Dancing in the Dark* [Lynx: Oxford, 1994]).

The deception intrinsic in this kind of double life is a straightforward denial of the truth. By living a lie we create an artificial world in which to indulge our fantasies. We ignore the awful damage that is the inevitable result. The simple fact is that God desires us to live the truth, not just to speak about it.

It is easy to look at such serious cases of moral failure and ignore our own sinful condition. Each one of us is quick to excuse those things that we think and do in private, which we would never want anyone else to be aware of. So often this is accompanied by a sense of deep regret, and a failure to recognise that secret sins will always produce a bitter harvest in our hearts and lives. Too often we have been guilty of seeking to avoid the truth.

Lies, damn lies

Lying is a universal sin (Ps 116:11; Jer 9:5). It is the product of deceitful hearts (Jer 17:9), and is condemned in Scripture (Ps 63:11; Rev 21:8). God specifically announces that he hates lies and loves the truth (Prov 12:22). His people are never to lie or to deceive each other (Lev 19:11; Col 3:9). Lying is denounced as the sin of Antichrist (1 Jn 2:22), and all habitual liars will inevitably forfeit the joys of eternal salvation (Rev 21:27).

At its root a lie is a statement of what is known to be false with intent to deceive (Judg 16:10, 13). Lies can be expressed in words (Prov 6:19), a way of life (Ps 62:9), error (2 Thess 2:11) or false religion (Rom 1:25). In the garden, the serpent deceived Eve by sowing doubt (Gen 3:1), then a lie (v 4) causing the man and woman to hide from God in fear (v 10).

The Old Testament prophets thundered their denunciation of lying as a specific expression of the principal of evil (Hos 12:1). It was incompatible with God's nature, and the moral conscience and social well-being of his people (Num 23:19; Ps 26:28; Prov 19:22). When truth is abused then false witness (Ex 20:16), fraud (Lev 6:2-3), wrong judgement (Deut 19:15) and false teaching (2 Tim 4:3) will result. God's people are therefore urged to stand firm for truth and to reject all falsehood (Eph 4:25; 6:14). Failure to do so, as in the case of Ananias and Sapphira, could produce awful consequences (Acts 5:1-10).

These sober warnings are there to encourage prevention rather than offer the provision of a cure. The good news is that free and full forgiveness is available for when we do sin, but this fact must never be employed as a licence for us to go on sinning (Rom 6:1-2).

We might reluctantly argue that lying is wrong, but that not all lies fall into the same category. Some lies are surely better than others?

Cain thought that he could escape with evading the truth (Gen 4:9), but nothing is hidden from the sight of God.

Abraham tried to tell a half-truth (Gen 12:10-20). Sarah may have been his wife, but she was also his half-sister. The pagan response was astonishment at such a deception!

Jacob lied to his father (Gen 27:19), and although he secured a blessing it was at the cost of years of exile.

In each of these cases human self-interest was at stake. It can be argued that Scripture does allow for a misimpression to be given. Samuel did not divulge his real reason for visiting Jesse and his sons at Bethlehem, but then he was under no obligation to do so (1 Sam 16:2).

In 1 Kings 22:20-23, God does permit a lying spirit to lure King Ahab to his doom. This subterfuge was to enable his righteous judgement on an evil king to be carried out.

God can override our misuse of truth, but only for the greater good, as in the case of Rahab the Jericho harlot (Josh 2:4-6). This can only be permitted by God's express will in special circumstances, and then only to fulfil his eternal purposes.

Our lies are intended to serve ourselves, and this is always condemned. Often our lies are well-intended and we feel they could be easily justified. A child is reluctant to shatter their parents illusions about them! A husband denies infidelity to spare his wife the pain of knowing the truth. Yet so often our lies become contagious – one builds on another – and eventual exposure is far more painful.

In our own family Ruth and I have always insisted to the children that we would rather know the truth. To lie is to make things worse. If trust is to exist in family life then a lie is the worst possible action – for it rarely stops at one!

Secret sins

Lies grow in the fertile soil of deceit. Instead of being something we say, they develop into a life that we live. Almost before we are aware of it we start living a lie.

It is easy to assume that no-one is quite as bad as ourselves! Often we are convinced that others are immune to the kind of temptations to which we so easily succumb. We fall into the trap of believing that if those who sit next to us in church knew what we were really like then they would move at least two seats away

from us! We attempt to conceal our weaknesses and failures –
which often results in them becoming larger and more prominent
in our lives.

Sadly, in today's society, large numbers of local churches are
waking up to the tragic reality that respected members of their
congregations are living a double life. Shock waves of surprise,
disappointment and sorrow greet the news that fellow-Christians
have been discovered living a lie, and no-one even suspected it.

Marital unfaithfulness, homosexual practice, misappropriation
of funds, child abuse, tax evasion, alcoholism, domestic violence
– the list appears to be endless. This tragic catalogue reflects sins
current in society, from which Christians have no immunity!

This list might, at first sight , represent quite an encouragement
to many of us. If we have never gone to these extremes we may
consider that we are not as bad as we at first thought. There is
some truth in this, and we should certainly seek to avoid
unnecessarily condemning ourselves.

Instead of condemning those who fail we should recognise that
it is only through God's grace and strength that we will avoid
doing the same kind of things.

We also run the risk of excusing those thoughts and
temptations which we harbour within ourselves, as if they were
any less dangerous. It is sometimes too easy to forget that
Scripture places selfish ambition alongside drunkenness, and
jealousy alongside sexual immorality in its list of prohibitions
(Rom 13:13; Gal 5:19-20).

The plain fact of the matter is that even the apostle Paul freely
admits to the struggle that goes on within us. He openly
acknowledged that we fail to live as we would wish, saying that,
'What I do is not the good I want to do; no, the evil I do not want
to do – this I keep on doing' (Rom 7:19).

If we are honest with ourselves we are each aware of the sinful
nature that exists within us. To fail to acknowledge this is only to
deceive ourselves (1 Jn 1:8). We all know of secret sins within us.
For as long as we blithely ignore them we run the risk that one day
they may overtake us. Instead of excusing our weaknesses we
need to guard each thought in order to make it obedient to Christ
(2 Cor 10:5). For in his death and risen life within us we can be set
free – even from our secret sins (Rom 6:18).

Danger – deceivers at play

One of the most disturbing results of discovering secret sin in the life of a fellow-Christian lies in the realisation that we have been deceived. To know what has taken place is traumatic enough. To realise that this has been going on over a period of time can be devastating.

Not only have we been deceived, the same will apply to many others. Indeed the person concerned may well have even been deceiving themselves.

We should not be too surprised. For the Christian life is a battle and many will be injured in the fight. We have an enemy of our souls who is longing to destroy Christians and discredit the church. Jesus called him 'the father of lies' (Jn 8:44), for from the very beginning he lied in the Garden.

Sometimes we can even be guilty of secretly rejoicing at the failures of others. This is totally unproductive – both for them, and for us. It is always best to regard someone with love and compassion, to view them as a casualty not a traitor!

A believer who actively practises deception is a hypocrite, and Jesus was unsparing in his condemnation of such pretence (Mt 6:2-5; 7:5; 15:7; 22:18; 23:13-29; Mk 12:5; Lk 12:56; 13:15). He recognised the existence of secret sin and warned that light exposes darkness, and reveals 'private sin' (Jn 3:20). In case people become proud of avoiding specific acts, he emphasised that a thought was sufficient to implicate them in this sinful practice (Mt 5:27-28).

Greek drama often employed the use of masks. An actor might play many parts in a performance, these would be differentiated by the use of a different mask. The Greek word *hypokritēs* means 'actor', someone fulfilling a role rather than being themselves. The original meaning was 'one who answers as in a dramatic dialogue'. It came to be used as a 'pretender', or someone who wore a mask to cover their true character. Such a person would be expert at putting on an external show while their inward thoughts and feelings were very different.

When Jesus denounced the hypocrisy of the scribes and Pharisees he used the Greek word *ouai*, 'woe to you' (Mt 23:13). This word contains a sense of wrath, but also of sorrow. Jesus rejects hypocrisy, but with a heart of love at their tragic failure to see that he longed to remove the mask and bring them into reality. That same desire still exists in his heart. For he knows who we are and longs to transform us into all that we could be.

The problem with initial deception is that it escalates, and exposure often involves the downfall of the person involved. Jesus likened hypocrisy to yeast – it spreads and infects the whole being (Lk 12:1). Consequently when sin and deception have been exposed they cannot just be ignored. To do so would damage the entire life of a church or fellowship. That unfashionable word 'discipline' has to be employed.

Nothing can be less pleasant for a local church than to be faced with the need to exercise correction and administer discipline. Fortunately, unlike the Old Testament days, we no longer have the responsibility for carrying out the death penalty! *The use of church discipline*

In meekness and humility discipline has to be exercised, first to the offender alone (Mt 18:15; Gal 6:1), then within the church (Mt 18:16; 1 Cor 5:5; 2 Cor 2:6). As a last resort the church must confront and even excommunicate the person involved (Mt 18:17; 1 Cor 5:5,13; 1 Tim 5:19-21).

This may sound harsh, but it is necessary for the well-being of the body of Christ. For obedience to the truth must be preserved. This is not to suggest that we should ever seek to act as an Inquisition, or as thought-police. Our intention is very different. God's truth will always survive, we do not have to fight in order to preserve it. Our responsibility is simply to safeguard our allegiance to that truth.

In confronting deception by discipline our intention should always be to achieve restoration, reconciliation and healing (Gal 6:1; Heb 12:5-11; Rev 3:19). God judges, chastises and punishes – but in order to bring people back to himself when they turn in repentance (1 Cor 11:29-32; 2 Cor 2:6-11). With the Lord Jesus there is *always* the potential for a second chance.

This is a continued emphasis in Scripture – Abraham, David, Elijah, Jonah, Moses, Thomas and Peter all failed God in a serious fashion. Yet each was to be subsequently used by God in a major way. Not only can we be restored, we can also be recommissioned for service. With God there is always a way back, and the promise of forgiveness and a fresh beginning.

Nobody's perfect

Jesus taught his disciples that when they prayed they should ask God to forgive them in exactly the same way that they forgave others (Mt 6:12; Lk 11:4).

The fact is that we all need forgiveness – often! It would be foolish to suggest that any one of us lives in the way that we would really wish. Each of us carries our secret imperfections and we need God to forgive us. We also damage others and need their forgiveness too. When we ourselves are the victims we need to forgive in similar fashion. Somehow we expect to be forgiven ourselves, but often find it hard to display the same attitude towards others.

It is difficult to overemphasise the awful feelings of betrayal at the discovery that someone has been living in a manner that discredits all of us. This is especially true if the person exercises a position of spiritual leadership. We can easily feel abused, the shocked and innocent victims – though never as innocent as we would wish others to believe!

When faced with this situation Jesus gives us no choice but to forgive. The exercise of this forgiveness is not to take the form of a weak-willed cop-out!

How should we forgive? It is easy to be tempted to either be over indulgent and too tolerant, or to be harsh and judgemental. We must be neither censorious nor sentimental. The biblical pattern is that we should confront, expose and subdue sinful practice among us. At the same time we should actively forgive and seek the reconciliation and restoration of the offending party. This is no weak concept, it takes strength to oppose sin, and even more to forgive the sinner (Lk 11:4; 17:4; Mk 11:25; Eph 4:32). Church leaders are responsible for caring for both those who sin and those sinned against. A difficult balance is called for that will ultimately be for the good of all concerned.

Whatever the degree of hurt we may feel, we remain under orders to 'forgive as the Lord forgave you' (Col 3:13).

The recognition that we are not all that we would want to be is fundamental to this process. Appreciating our own weaknesses can help us to anticipate them in others. It is here that honesty, sharing and mutual help comes into play.

We have not been called by God to live an isolated Christian existence. Instead we are instructed to encourage and support each other, literally to 'love one another' within the body of Christ (1 Thess 4:18; 5:11; Tit 2:6; Heb 3:13; 10:25; 1 Jn 4:11). As John reminded his readers, 'anyone who does not love his brother, whom he has seen, cannot love God, whom he has not seen'. And he has given us this command: 'Whoever loves God must also love his brother' (1 Jn 4:20-21).

The need for encouragement

If we open up ourselves and become vulnerable to Christian friends, we can receive the help and support we need. We were never intended to cope alone, but with the encouragement of one another. In such a situation we must be careful never to betray any trust or confidence, but to offer mutual support and encouragement. The desire is that we might learn as God's people to be friends together. It is out of such relationships, as David found with Jonathan, and Ruth with Naomi, that trust and openness can grow.

There are many who feel threatened at the mere suggestion of such honesty. 'What if?' or 'Yes, but' are normal responses. Some of us have been so 'closed-off' for years that we find it hard to contemplate what people would really think of us if we allowed them to peer behind the mask.

The familiar question to the children of the sixties and beyond is this: 'What is truth in terms of personal behaviour?' We readily ask, 'Where is the real me?' The Christian response is that the real me is the one God knows and Jesus died for. He knows us as we really are and we only truly discover ourselves as we give our lives to him. It is then that we uncover our true potential, and are released to live in reality.

Truth is no mere academic process. Knowing the truth involves discovering the truth about each other. We may worry that as soon as we peel away the veneer of our public character, then someone will discover the chipboard underneath. This is true, but honesty can be really liberating. Truth releases us, and greater honesty about ourselves will often result in others following our example. As

Knowing the truth about each other

superficiality is dispelled we can aid each other in addressing areas of tension and problem in our lives.

Few spiritual failures just occur overnight! It is usually preceded by an extended period of temptation building up towards the sin that eventually occurs. Usually it will be located in an area of inherent weakness, what the Puritans termed a 'besetting sin'.

Each of us is aware of areas in our lives which we find particularly difficult. For some this disposition may be toward anger, for others towards bitterness, avarice or lust. It is in this particular area that we need to exercise the most care. Here we need protection, love and support – but it is the last area of our lives that we would ever reveal to others!

The suggestion is not that we should spend our lives sharing personal weaknesses and temptations with each other. It is that we should develop trust and respect with particular friends. Together we can help each other make progress in God – and not fall! Rather than find that we shock each other, we may be surprised to find the level of mutual understanding that is swiftly achieved.

Walking in the Light God is described as light – a potent picture of openness and honesty, as well as purity. We deceive ourselves if we think we can live in sin and deceit and maintain a relationship with him (1 Jn 1:6). We are called to walk in the light, nothing hidden in a dark corner of our being, as if we can conceal anything from our all-knowing God!

This open relationship with God is the solid basis for our open relationship with fellow believers (1 Jn 1:7). To maintain and develop these valuable relationships, openness must be mutual and predicated on continually maintaining the partners' relationships with God. Our capacity for self-deception is great. Cultivating transparent friendship with someone of the same sex, for mutual accountability, can help us see our inconsistencies and blind spots, and act as incentive to spiritual fidelity and growth. Many Christian leaders have found this type of relationship a great safeguard from temptation, and support in troubled times.

Yet is honesty enough? For honesty without faith is defeatist and depressing, while faith without honesty is unreal and intimidating. If someone pours out their hearts to us with a catalogue of woes and weaknesses, it is scarcely an edifying experience! If they do so in anticipation that together, as we move on in God, we are going to see his triumph and victory at work in our lives, then that is a significant moment.

This is the context of genuine fellowship. The breakdown of reserve and creation of mutual support has become of inestimable value to those who seek to live in the truth of who they are. By acknowledging our own imperfections and accepting the reality of others, we acquire the means to support and encourage each other.

The missing word

Every society needs its scapegoats. In cricket it is the captain, in football the manager, in politics the Prime Minister, and in the church it is the leadership. Often the responsibility is regarded by its recipients as outweighing the privilege! For the leaders can often find themselves blamed for everything.

Leadership is a firmly biblical concept. True leaders are chosen by God (Hag 2:23; Acts 9:15), they are to be humble (Ex 3:11; Judg 6:15; 1 Sam 18:18; Mt 3:14), courageous (1 Kings 22:30; Acts 4:18-20; 7:51), and incorruptible (1 Kings 13:8; 2 Kings 5:15-17; Dan 5:17). They are also liable to more severe examination and judgement by God. Their standards are to be proportionally higher than those required of their people (Ezek 34:2; 2 Pet 2:1-3; Jude:12; Jas 3:1).

Leaders are to set an example for the believers in their conduct, speech, love and faith. They are to live in purity, teaching and preaching the truth of God (1 Tim 3:1; 4:12-13). They are to be self-controlled, blameless and above reproach, holding firm to the truth and refuting those who oppose it (Tit 1:6-9).

Therefore when a church leader fails, the shock waves reverberate through the congregation. Imagine how a young man felt when he discovered that the minister who had preached at his wife's funeral was having an affair at the time. Such things – and worse – actually happen. Frequently leaders believe it could never happen to them, and then it does.

The missing word is 'integrity'. As leaders, many of us assume a special-case mentality. We excuse our failures on grounds of pressure, stress or the

Leaders need to be open about themselves

unreasonable expectations of our people. We hide behind the persona of 'leader' and try to ensure that no-one can see us as we really are.

As a child I was always afraid of going to heaven. I was under the illusion that eternity would be spent listening to God reading from a library of big, black books. Inside them would be recorded all that each individual had ever done in their lives. My reluctance to be there stemmed from the fact that my dad would be in heaven. When God arrived at my name, dad would learn the truth of all that I had done, that he never knew about, and I would be deeply ashamed.

As a man I similarly tried to hide from others the weaknesses I possessed, and too often indulged in. The liberating truth finally dawned on me that my wife Ruth, and friends like Lyndon Bowring, Mike Morris and Dave Pope did know what I was really like, but remained friends!

The great value of friendship   Pretence has slowly disappeared as I have learned the faithfulness of friendship. Meeting together, three or four times a year with a bunch of special friends, to share and pray, has been an amazing revelation to me. Nothing has remained hidden as we have tried to help and support each other. The fact that these times, taken from busy diaries, have continued for over thirteen years is a miracle in itself.

At a personal level I freely confess that the value of this group has been inestimable. Ruth and I have been really privileged in the friends God had given us. The pastoral support of Alex and Peggy Buchanan and Roger and Faith Forster, a small support group of trusted advisers, and a host of informal friends have been a lifeline for us. In the sometimes turbulent world of seeking to represent evangelical Christians within secular society we have needed our friends – and God has provided us with such special people that we are deeply grateful.

In learning to give time to family I have also needed to discover the importance of being among friends. As an only child, and an intensely private person, this has been the context in which God has slowly peeled away the layers of what I want people to think I am, in order to expose the real me. This has not always been a comfortable process. Several years ago Graham Kendrick commented to me, 'I don't trust you Clive, you think too fast, work out too much, see too far ahead with that devious mind of yours – but I do trust God in you.'

Comments like that may seem destructive; but not in the context of trusted friendship. The value of Graham's comment was that it helped me to face up to how others viewed me, and to appreciate that God was at work in my life.

Scripture observes that, 'Wounds from a friend can be trusted' (Prov 27:6). We all need friends who know how to be straight and honest with us, who have our best interests at heart, and are 'rooting for us'.

In the light of the tragic current spate of moral failures appearing to reach epidemic proportions we need to ask how we can help each other avoid the pitfalls which have resulted in this sad situation.

The first essential requirement is that we are prepared to be honest with others. I freely concede *Be honest with one another* that I doubt very much if I would still be in Christian ministry today were it not for my wife, children and my friends.

For too long we have lived with the myth of self-confident leadership. Rarely is this true, and when it is it can rarely be helpful. If any of us become isolated little islands in a vast and lonely sea we are unlikely to be of much relational value to others.

One real sign of hope on the spiritual horizon is the relative absence of competitiveness among itinerant Christian leaders. Once this group was renowned for independence and self-serving; now there seems to have emerged a large informal network of co-operative and mutual care. Many have a small group of trusted friends to meet with them. Others look to a 'spiritual director'. There is no reason why these helpful practices should be confined to leaders.

An old tradition records an unwritten saying of Jesus about the Pharisees, the religious leaders of his day. He is reported as saying 'The key of the kingdom they hid' (cf Mt 23:13). In failing to enter the kingdom themselves, they shut the door on others as well. Our duty is to practise the opposite. To have the integrity to 'walk our talk', seeking to live up to the message we preach – and helping each other to do so.

Truth never simply exists in a vacuum. It is there to release and bring life. As those who have heard and responded to the truth, we have a God-given duty to live up to its demands. The apostle Paul talks of us being good soldiers for our commanding officer (2 Tim 2:3-6). As such we need to avoid conduct unbecoming of soldiers of Jesus Christ.

Be honest with God Whatever we may do to try to hide, we can never escape the gaze of God. There is never any point in being other than honest with God, because he knows us better than we know ourselves (Ps 139:1-4, 23-24). Jesus lived a human life and knows exactly what it is like to be faced by temptation – he understands us from the inside (Heb 4:15-16). Prayer is therefore no optional extra. For we can draw on this great spiritual resource. Whenever we drift towards danger we can talk to the One who knows us as we are – and still loves us.

When we are honest with God we can begin to receive help and support to avoid 'conduct unbecoming'. He provides all the forgiveness and strength we need (1 Jn 1:8-9). It is because God is there, he is not distant but here with us, that truth is objective not subjective. If we were alone we could determine our own destiny. Because he is here we can live as he intends, but we need the help of one another, and supremely of the Holy Spirit.

In the final analysis we need to build honesty and trust through personal friendship, which will help us avoid the cycle of deceit and shock. This will not always work, but it will certainly help. And we need to practise forgiveness in such a way that the world will recognise the reality of Christian love and restoration (Jn 13:34-35). We may not always avoid sinning, but we can help each other to start again!

The plain fact of the matter is that sins can be cleansed. Life can restart and God will be glorified through forgiven sinners who have come to know and live by his truth.

10

Battle for the Truth

This last chapter examines the opposition we face: Satan, and his lies expressed in philosophy and elsewhere. We have a duty as Christians to think clearly, to perceive the truth, and to announce it boldly.

Battle for the Truth

Error is none the better for being common, nor
truth worse for having lain neglected.

John Locke.

Nine...ten...out!
Yes, this is the last chapter, but there is more to the use of the boxing countdown than that. Some people enjoy a fight, others object to the very idea. We enjoy the tranquillity of a more peaceful existence. However, the church is engaged in a life-threatening battle for truth. The tragedy is that few Christians even realise it!

It is only when we are committed to truth, and are prepared to search for and establish it, that we will remove abuse.

The story is told of a history lesson delivered by a Nazi official at a labour camp. He explained that 'The Jesuits were originally a savage Indian tribe, who emigrated very early in history to Spain via Arabia, and settled down in Northern Spain where they were made Catholics. For their savage and unscrupulous fierceness, the Popes took them into their service as the church's vanguard. How disastrous they proved for Germany is clearly proved by the historical fact that it was the Jesuits who urged Charlemagne to the merciless massacre of the Saxons at Verden.'

175

We may laugh at how people could be so misled. The distortion of truth through advertising or propaganda is well known. What is less recognised is the subtle manner in which concepts of absolute truth have been discredited over recent years.

No longer is truth regarded as a secure concept. Part of the uniqueness of our humanity lies in an intuitive sense of right and wrong. Yet we are constantly being reassured that what we previously assumed was wrong could be right, if not for us, then perhaps for someone else.

This uncertainty has not only been fostered by philosophy, it is also endemic within the arts. The impact of surrealism, with artists like Salvador Dali, writers like Samuel Beckett, the music of John Cage, and the theatre of the absurd, have all seriously undermined the concept of objective truth.

We are encouraged to believe that what is truth for us, may not be truth for someone else, and we certainly have no right to inflict our truth on others. The idea that truth might be true for everyone is dismissed. True truth is no longer an acceptable concept.

The erosion of society's security base... Earlier in the century society found its security in the traditional pillars of government, the church, the process of law and the Press. Today, that trust and confidence in the reliability of these institutions has been drastically eroded.

...the monarchy... While politicians have always been treated with a measure of cynical disregard, the monarchy has retained the confidence and affection of many people. Since the reign of Queen Victoria, the Royal Family has gained increasing popularity and been regarded as a strong bulwark of staunch family life and high moral values. With the notable exception of the monarch herself, and the Queen Mother, this idealised portrait has been sadly marred by a procession of allegations. Adultery, divorce and deception have grabbed the headlines. The model family has been smashed beyond recognition and the pain is etched vividly upon the features of a well-respected monarch.

...justice... Once British justice was universally regarded as the best in the world. Truth, most people felt, was to be found in a courtroom. Today, allegations of police corruption and the miscarriage of justice have gravely tarnished that reputation.

Traditional respect for our legal system and law enforcement agency has survived – but not unscathed.

We must never deny the sincerity and integrity of the majority of those involved. We must be grateful to God for their dedication and commitment. However, we must also recognise that popular understanding of truth has been damaged by this growing sense of disenchantment with the process of law.

At worst, the critic dismisses the issue in the cynical phrase, 'You get the justice you can afford'. At best, justice has often become popularly regarded as that which survives the legal rhetoric. 'The truth, the whole truth' refers to that evidence which survives the attacks of clever lawyers. No longer can truth be regarded as secure in a courtroom, or when read from a police statement.

While popular confidence in politicians has never *...and politics* been particularly high, accusations of sleaze, impropriety and lack of integrity have further tarnished an already soiled public image.

Such judgements may well be both harsh and unfair, but they represent a rising tide of public opinion. The old certainties are gone, established institutions have become suspect, and many have resorted to the safety of a fantasy world. The plastic world of the soap opera has replaced the plain truth of everyday life.

Materialistic ideas of self-advancement and hedonistic pleasures of self-indulgence have almost obliterated a benevolent concern for others and an unselfish passion for truth.

While it is doubtful if many lived solely for truth in the past, at least there was clarity over what it was. Today we drift on a tide of uncertainty into a sea of unknowing – and we have lost our anchor! For active commitment to God has become more marginal than an acceptance of objective truth.

It is possible to devise all kinds of rational explanations as to why this has taken place. The Christian response is to reiterate that truth to follow is revealed in Scripture, and truth for living is found in Jesus. To assert otherwise is to deny the Christian faith. Reluctantly we have to conclude that an enemy has done this!

The father of lies

Another unfashionable notion is that there might actually be an author of pain, deceit and evil. The Bible has no such reservations. It clearly depicts Satan as the adversary of Jesus and the prince of all evil (Num 22:22).

Jesus is the incarnation of truth, but Satan remains the embodiment of falsehood and for that reason is denounced as the 'father of lies' (Jn 8:44).

The father of lies The devil began life as a created being, an angel of God who was powerful, moral, attractive and wise (Ezek 28:12-17). Unwilling to remain as the chief administrator of created beings, Satan attempted to seize the reins of universal government. He wanted to be God and challenged the divine authority. As a direct result of this rebellion Satan and those angels which supported him were ejected from heaven to make their home in hell (Isa 14:12; 1 Tim 3:6; Jude:6). He now rules as king of the demons. His uncanny subtlety enables him to employ his armies to fulfil his own tricks and strategies which are aimed directly at undermining God and his truth.

Satan employs violence, deception, intrigue and deceit in order to attack God's purposes for his created order (Gen 3:1-19; Mk 5:3; Lk 4:9-10). He invades people's lives, casts doubt on God's truth, and attempts to counterfeit divine activities (Gen 3:1- 5; Lk 22:3; Jn 13:27; 2 Thess 2:9).

Satan is a menace, and never more than when on his home territory of deceit. He knows how to employ lies for his own ends, and this practice is therefore expressly condemned within Scripture.

Lies can be used in several different ways, to:

* Justify error (2 Thess 2:11).
* Perpetuate fraud (Lev 6:2-3).
* Obtain a wrongful condemnation (Deut 19:15).
* Support false forms of religion (Rom 1:25). Words, lifestyle, false prophecy can all be employed to put forward that which is false with intention to deceive (Judg 16:10, 13; Prov 6:19; Ps 62:9; Jer 14:4).

The Oxford academic C. S. Lewis wisely observed that the greatest lie that Satan has succeeded in perpetuating is to persuade humankind that:

> There are two equal and opposite errors into which our race can fall about the devils. One is to disbelieve in their existence. The other is to believe, and to feel an excessive and unhealthy interest in them. They themselves are equally pleased by both errors and hail a materialist or a magician with the same delight. (C. S. Lewis, *The Screwtape Letters* [Collins: Glasgow 1942]).

While the Christian mind has often devoted too much attention to Satan and his accompanying forces, secular society has stubbornly refused to even acknowledge his existence. The modern mind finds it almost impossible to believe that Satan could be real, let alone the actual embodiment of falsehood within our world.

Many cogent and powerful reasons undergird this contemporary reluctance. Satan is a spirit, in a world which excludes spiritual forces from both conversation and belief. He is worshipped by a perceived lunatic fringe of satanists which make him unworthy of serious attention. Because he is non-material he is intellectually indefensible. He is evil, and modern western culture resolutely refuses to believe in the existence of evil.

Instead people blame human imperfection, malicious fate, or cosmic mistakes for the malaise that grips our world and the disasters which we frequently endure. Alternatively, they attribute malice or injustice to God himself.

The biblical version of events is very different. *The reality* Scripture unequivocally recognises the existence of a *of evil* malevolent and personal devil who employs lying spirits in his endeavours to pervert and destroy the truth (1 Kings 22:22-23; 2 Chron 18:21-22).

This same Satan assaults human minds with doubts, fear and propaganda (Gen 3:1-5; Mt 16:22-23; Mk 5:36; Acts 9:26; 1 Jn 4:18). Through pride he fell from heaven (Isa 14:12; 1 Tim 3:6) and now besieges human spirits with lust, pride and hatred (Eph 2:2-3; Gal 5:19-21). He attacks human bodies with disease, torture and death (Lk 12:4-5; 13:11-16; Mk 5:1-15). He attempts to invade human nations with structural evil (Rev 2:13).

Satan is therefore the very antithesis of the truth. Yet falsehood was to be vanquished by truth nailed to a cross. For even in his own territory of death Satan was defeated by One who died by choice and then rose from the dead (Col 2:15). This triumph of Jesus confirmed the sentence passed on Satan in the Garden of Eden. It proved that he had been dispossessed by one stronger than himself, and that his destiny was assured (Mk 3:27).

He is therefore confined to the earth. As merely a fallen angel he is limited in time, space and power.

The only prospect Satan faces is of judgement by fire, for him and his demonic supporters (Mt 25:41; Rev 20:10). Their time is fast running out – truth has triumphed.

Falsehood and evil, therefore, already lie defeated. Satan can only exercise his activity within the limits that God lays down, and he may even find himself unconsciously used to forward the course of truth! (Job 1:12; 2:6; 1 Cor 5:5; 10:13; 2 Cor 12:7; Rev 20:2, 7).

Satan may be a malignant reality, always hostile to the truth, but God's people are able to resist him (Jas 4:7). Many fail to recognise that a battle has even taken place, but at the end of the age Satan's defeat by the truth will be obvious for all to see.

A matter of philosophy

If deception appeared today with a forked tail and slimy appearance, then no-one would have any doubt to its origins. Sadly for us it assumes a far more sophisticated guise. Doubts as to the possibility of absolute truth existing have emerged from thinkers and scholars. These influencers have themselves been influenced.

There may be nothing intrinsically wrong with philosophy, but as the study of human wisdom it is here that the root of truth-destructive wisdom began.

For a philosopher, a liar is a man who has wilfully misplaced his ontological predicates. In other words he says what he does not believe.

Modern western thought is linear. We think in straight lines. This Greek habit of thought is clearly illustrated by Aristotle's definition of truth, 'to say of what is that it is, and of what is not that it is not, is true.' This simple statement forms the basis for our traditional secular understanding of this subject.

Aristotle's definition of truth

Great thinkers like Augustine, Aquinas, Descartes and Spinoza maintained that truth is conceived as an agreement between the mind and reality. Falsehood was the reverse, and as Aquinas commented, 'any intellect which understands a thing to be otherwise than it is, is false.'

Aquinas felt that natural and artificial things have truth in relation to the intellect on which they depend. This is where God comes in, for the divine and human intellects are not the same. God is the primal truth. He is the principle and source which Augustine saw as prompting our own inner voice to confirm truth. Indeed, for Spinoza, the truth of an idea depended on its relation to God.

It was his view of God as both the originator and origin of truth that gave Aquinas his two-step process in presenting the case for Christianity. He used philosophical arguments to lay the foundations, then completed the job with Christian teachings. For Aquinas all truth came from God, so it could be uncovered in philosophy and theology alike.

Aquinas' use of philosophy

The rationalist Descartes based his method on mathematics. His famous saying, *Cogito ergo sum*, 'I think, therefore I am,' declared where he was coming from. He determined to accept as true only that which he knew to be true. Since God, to be God, had to be perfect, he could not deceive us. We could therefore trust our logical deductions about reality, for he would not allow us to think that our clear and distinct ideas were true if, in fact, they were false.

Change was to arrive with the Enlightenment. Locke pointed out that verbal and real truth are not necessarily the same thing. 'Though our words signify nothing but our ideas, yet being designed by them to signify things, the truth they contain, when put into propositions, will be only verbal, when they stand for ideas in the mind that have not an agreement with the reality of things.'

The idea of truth in the Enlightenment

This concept was put in simpler form by Dr Johnson when he pointed out that offering our own sincere convictions gives no guarantee of their accuracy. So he distinguished between *moral* truth, where we say what we mean, and *physical* truth, where we declare what is actually the case.

Hume and secular scepticism   Locke distinguished between faith and reason. He accepted that which lay beyond human reason as coming from God himself. With Hume arrived the classic expression of secular scepticism about truth. He determined that human reason could prove neither the existence of external things or oneself. It is not surprising to record that one truth he swiftly discarded was the existence of miracles. He argued that miracles were impossible because they were violations of the laws of nature, and these laws were, by definition, inviolable. Hume urged that miracles therefore could never be used to establish faith, but could only be swallowed by those who already had sufficient faith to believe them.

Kant was to go further. He considered truth to consist in

For Kant truth could not be universal   'the accordance of a cognition with its object'. So a universal criterion of truth is impossible. He also distinguished between the truth which a proposition has when it conforms to the rules of thought adopted, and the intrinsic truth it possesses when it represents nature.

Kant concluded that a single idea, of itself, cannot be true or false. In this he disagreed with Spinoza, but like Aristotle, Descartes and Locke believed that a simple idea could never be straightforwardly judged as right or wrong. He put it like this, 'truth and error... are only to be found in a judgement...the senses do not err, not because they always judge correctly, but because *they do not judge at all.*'

Kant believed that all knowledge begins with experience, truth was a very individual perspective.

Truth and expediency   Pragmatism arrived from North America in the latter part of the nineteenth century. Followers of this position adopted terms like, 'Truth is what works', 'The true is the expedient', and 'Faith in a fact helps create the fact'.

From the work of William James came the simple belief that '"the true" is only the expedient in the way of our thinking, just as 'the right' is only the expedient in the way of our behaving.'

The Pragmatist school of thought declared that the sole test of truth lay in its consequences. Truth was therefore not absolute, it was relative to each individual and situation. They assumed that God was a mere working hypothesis bearing no relation to facts, ignoring the Christian insistence that their faith is not simply based upon experience.

Twentieth-century thought has been dominated by attempts to understand the relationship of language to truth. These owe their roots to the work of Hume and the Pragmatists, so it is largely sceptical and relativistic in its initial approach.

The approach of Logical Positivism was dominant until the 1960s. Antagonistic to discourse about God which it regarded as unscientific, illogical and nonsensical, its exponents included A. J. Ayer and Anthony Flew.

Logical positivism

They hold what most of us would regard as factual statements as purely emotional and individualistic utterances in disguise. So a statement like 'stealing is wrong' does not refer to a divine command, but means 'I disapprove of stealing". Religious truth is dismissed because, in their words, 'What cannot logically be demonstrated cannot be logically said.'

In contrast, the more recent work of Ludwig Wittgenstein, J. L. Austin and others has claimed that words like 'I love you' can work perfectly well without being logically verifiable. This school of Ordinary Language Philosophy holds that the truth of all statements is only relative to their context and usage. So 'The truth is what works.'

The currently popular post-structuralist school views language as self-referential. Associated with scholars like Roland Barthes and Jacques Derrido, they maintain that the system of language is the sum total of reality, while Christians would want to affirm that there is a Word above all words.

This philosophical speculation may not make for easy reading, but it is vital if we are to gain a proper understanding as to why society thinks as it does. For these ideas have permeated the understanding of the communicators of our generation. They are then regurgitated in a form that subverts the concept of truth that Christians seek to maintain.

These ideas subvert the Christian concept of truth

The purpose statement of the Free University of Brussels openly acknowledges that it is 'searching for all truth, but denying revealed truth.' In other words, truth cannot be accepted if its origin is not human.

Meanwhile, the commodification of truth has become complete. Truth is changed with each mask the actor disgards. Madonna changes her image and her role at will. We each become our own truth in whatever guise we currently choose to adopt. Truth is the image we buy for ourselves.

While there is no conscious conspiracy at work, the denigration of concepts of absolute truth, and the variety of substitutes we choose for ourselves, represents a real threat to truth as the Church once proclaimed it to be.

Blind to the truth?

Faced with popular dismissal of the Christian view of truth, the church must take action on behalf of its people. For we are not immune to the pressures presented by our culture.

Some Christians have simply withdrawn from society. We have privatised our own morality, maintaining its validity for Christians, while ignoring the dire consequences for everyone else.

Others have given way to doubt and fear. Feeling that our beliefs are no longer tenable, we compromise with our culture, giving way on issues like homosexual practice which Scripture has explicitly forbidden. Fearing the rejection of neighbours, colleagues and society, we have failed to take a stand for truth.

It was said of King Solomon that his sensuality with his wives and concubines turned his heart from God (1 Kings 11:3-4). It is possible for us to be similarly distracted, compromising truth in order to enjoy our own pleasure-based existence.

Taking a stand for truth – the task we shirk Instead of concentrating on 'truth issues' which affect society, Christians have often been content with arguing over the minutiae of church doctrine and practice. By 'majoring on minors' and looking at issues that are largely irrelevant to the majority of society, we have stolen time from more important issues. When one looks today at the work of CARE and other bodies, we have to ask what we were concentrating on when abortion law reform was first suggested in 1966. Now we do good work – but too late!

Meanwhile society is led into killing truth by degrees. Point by point critical issues of truth like euthanasia, family values, and justice towards the two-thirds world, are addressed in an ethical framework far removed from Christian truth. As Christians we have to be committed to the preservation of life and to resisting oppression and injustice. For too long we were more concerned over whether or not one should raise holy hands in worship! This may be important, and of concern to us, but it will never address the real issues in society today.

For as long as we proceed in this direction, Satan smiles. He hates the truth because it is liberating. His desire is that we should keep it strictly to ourselves. We have no right to co-operate with the enemy of our souls!

Truth can never be selfish. Those who receive its benefits place themselves under an obligation to transmit the message to others. Those who have met God's truth in Jesus cannot justify remaining silent about him. Truth is not given to be restricted or contained. Instead it is designed to be given away.

Our belief in the existence of God must also never be divorced from our understanding of truth. Each practice needs to be examined in order that we never contradict Scripture by what we do. This applies to the way we treat each other. John taught us to 'walk in the light', and have fellowship with each other (1 Jn 1:7). This means that we need to be open and vulnerable to others, and offer and receive help and friendship, to hold each other in the truth.

In our worship we cannot ignore our theology. It is good to see a growing commitment to the expression of truth in the songs that we sing. While society urges us to do and say that which comes naturally, our commitment to truth demands that we hold our doctrine and practice in harmony.

The spirit of our age can too easily shine through our evangelistic methods and message. We invite people to a better life, when Jesus offered life as alone it should be lived. We share good news of satisfaction, fulfilment and all we need for life. This may be true, but Jesus brought good news of hard times, discipleship, suffering, persecution and even death. This is the

Christianity is not a cheap gospel flip side of the gospel – but we omit it at our peril. We dare not compromise the truth by sharing a 'cheap gospel'. People are looking for reality, and following the truth does not excuse us from difficulties. It does offer a God who takes us through them in the way that truth alone can do.

If we only preach the benefits of Christianity, we prejudice the integrity of our message. The simple gospel containing the propositional truth of Jesus is quite adequate – it does not need to be marked as a bargain offer! Whether in the office, pulpit, or over a cup of coffee, we need to recognise the hallmark of Christianity as repentance and faith, rather than material success. For the gospel is not just relatively better – it is absolutely true!

We must not be blind to truth in our witness, fellowship, evangelism, worship or lifestyle. God's truth must always be the arbiter in all that we do.

Falsehood, deception, lying and loss of integrity are explicitly denounced by Scripture (Lev 19:11; Ps 5:6; 63:11; 101:7; Prov 19:5; 21:6; Is 44:25; Col 3:9). Rather than turn a blind eye to our weaknesses, we must confront them honestly in ourselves, and lovingly in each other – for the sake of the truth.

The truth marches on

This is a focus that we have to regain, and much has changed for the good in recent years. We have lived through a generation where the emphasis has been on experiencing the truth. This has been good, for truth is to be known, not just thought. Having rediscovered enthusiasm and joy in the truth we must now find a right balance between experience and the content of our faith.

Hear the call: Christians should return to scholarship The call originally made by John Stott in the 1950's for Christians to return to scholarship is being heeded. Over fifty percent of Church of England ordinands in training are evangelicals, and the figure for the Church of Scotland is even higher. This can only be good news, for it shows that the section of the church most committed to experience is also working at its theology.

When my oldest daughter Vicky announced that she had a

place at Durham University to read Theology I was delighted. Others were less pleased. Warnings were given of vast numbers of theological students losing their faith through studying the subject. Yet we have to be prepared to grapple with difficult issues – in that way our faith gets stronger!

Similarly, many are disturbed at the idea of other religions being taught in school alongside Christianity. The alternative is to adopt a policy of no religious teaching at all. Then Sociology, Politics and History will still be taught, but not Religious Studies. Why should we fear our children gaining information about other faiths? If Jesus is the truth, then we need not be afraid, the truth will triumph.

A much better answer to the dilemma is to recruit more Christian governors, teachers and SACRE members – to raise the quality of teaching and syllabus, and to preserve the field of religious education.

The growth of correspondence courses, opportunities for college education, the lectures and programmes of Christian Impact, the Cambridge Papers, and many other tools for building a Christian response to contemporary issues has been vitally significant.

Fresh emphasis on apologetics and study has raised our awareness of the need to relate Christian faith to secular society. Meanwhile, the growth of opportunities to express Christian truth on the media and in the Press has further confirmed the relevance of Peter's injunction 'Always be prepared to give an answer to everyone who asks you to give the reason for the hope that you have ' (1 Pet 3:15).

The words that follow also need to be taken to heart. We need to remind our world of the truth that Jesus has entrusted to us 'with gentleness and respect' (1 Pet 3:15). Jesus was unsparing in his condemnation of hypocrisy and unrelenting in his proclamation of truth. His is the example that we need to follow.

While society announces that each can choose their own way, Christians have to announce the uniqueness of Jesus, and the exclusiveness of his message.

We live among people who have been 'robbed of the truth' (1 Tim 6:5). Many have lost any reverence for truth and have 'wandered away from the truth' (2 Tim 2:18). They have turned away from it, rejected and denied the truth (2 Tim 4:4; Tit 1:14; Jas 3:14). Others are 'always learning but never knowing the truth' (2 Tim 3:7), and some even 'oppose the truth' (2 Tim 3:8). How can we go on sinning after knowing the truth (Heb 10:26)? God wants to bring us back to the truth (Jas 5:19, 2 Tim 2:25).

This is the simple truth – once we have found it in Jesus, we need to boldly announce it to a world that remains deceived in the absence of truth.

Our longing remains that of Jesus, 'Then you will know the truth, and the truth will set you free' (Jn 8:32).

Further Reading

God In The Wasteland
David F. Wells, IVP, (Leicester, 1994)

A startling challenge to contemporary Christianity, this book exposes the extent of the corruption of modern evangelicalism by modernity. The author seeks to re-emphasise God's transcendence in the face of an over-emphasis on God's immanence. Wells argues that God's 'truth is too distant, his grace is too ordinary, his judgement is too benign, his gospel is too easy and his Christ is too common.' This is not just a book that analyses our problems, it happily points us to some of the answers.

Know The Truth
Bruce Milne, IVP (Leicester, 1982)

Too few Christians today know what they believe or why they believe it. Every mature Christian should have a book of basic doctrine which they can refer to regularly. This book gives an overview of evangelical belief in a clear, concise and challenging way. It will instruct and enlighten. Read it, study it, continually refer to it. *Know The Truth* is an invaluable reference tool which should provoke the reader to further study the Scriptures to find truth.

The Glory Of Christ
Peter Lewis, Hodder & Stoughton (London, 1992)

Set against current concerns, this masterly treatment of the person and work of Christ represents the best of popular theology. Pastorally sensitive and theologically aware, *The Glory Of Christ* inspires devotion to Christ through its clear teaching. It warms the heart and stretches the mind. It is thoroughly biblical and succeeds in addressing the major contemporary challenges to the traditional Christian belief in Jesus as Lord and Christ in a way that everyone can understand.

Dissonant Voices
Harold H. Netland, Apollos/IVP (Leicester, 1991)

Christian claims that Jesus is *the* way to God have been assaulted from all sides. This scholarly work gives a cogent defence of Christian exclusivism, responding to those attacks from within and without the Church. Moving from philosophic and religious issues the author focuses on Christ and concludes with a valuable discussion of evangelism, dialogue and tolerance. Religious pluralism is the greatest challenge facing evangelicalism in the final years of the twentieth century: *Dissonant Voices* helps us meet that challenge.

The Moral Maze
David Cook, SPCK (London, 1983)

In a world of compromise and the shifting sand of ethical uncertainty, the claim of Scripture to instruct us on matters of right and wrong is hotly disputed. How should Christians make right ethical choices? *The Moral Maze* guides the reader through the minefield of moral philosophy and contemporary thinking in a clear, thoughtful and practical way. Christians too often seek simplistic answers to complex problems without the discipline of understanding why the biblical way is the authoritative answer. David Cook's excellent and readable book shows us how to apply the truth of Scripture to modern ethical dilemmas. It will help set your feet on solid ground. A must for all Christians confronting ethical issues.